MORMONISM
FOR BEGINNERS®

D0756962

MORMONISM
FOR BEGINNERS®

BY STEPHEN CARTER • ILLUSTRATIONS BY JETT ATWOOD

Foreword by Jana Riess

FOR BEGINNERS®

For Beginners LLC
155 Main Street, Suite 211
Danbury, CT 06810 USA
www.forbeginnersbooks.com

Text: © 2016 Stephen Carter
Illustrations: © 2016 Jett Atwood

A For Beginners® Documentary Comic Book

Copyright © 2016

Cataloging-in-Publication information is
available from the Library of Congress.

ISBN-13 # 978-1-939994-52-3 Trade

Manufactured in the United States of America

For Beginners® and Beginners Documentary
Comic Books® are published
by For Beginners LLC.
First Edition

10 9 8 7 6 5 4 3 2 1

Note on sources and citations:
Passages quoted from Mormon scripture and
other LDS documents are cited as follows:
Doctrine and Covenants—D&C section:verse
*History of the Church of Jesus Christ of Latter-day
Saints*—HC volume:page
Joseph Smith–History (in The Pearl of Great
Price)—History chapter: verse
Book of Moses (in The Pearl of Great Price)—Moses chapter:verse
Book of Abraham (in The Pearl of Great
Price)—Abraham chapter:verse
Book of Moroni (in The Book of Mormon)—Moroni chapter:verse
Second Book of Nephi (in The Book of
Mormon—2 Nephi chapter:verse
Book of Ether (in The Book of Mormon—Ether chapter:verse
All other books and periodicals are cited by
title and edition, where appropriate.

For Eugene England

Thanks to the friends who, in addition to saving me from the jaws of error, also added details and insights to this book: Scot Denhalter, James Goldberg, John Hatch, Blair Hodges, Lindsay Hansen Park, Ardis Parshall, Dallas Robbins, Ethan Sproat, Brian Stuy, and Dan Wotherspoon.

CONTENTS

Foreword

by Jana Riess

I t's a religion! It's a subculture! It's a Broadway show!

All three of those exclamations hold true for the Church of Jesus Christ of Latter-day Saints, commonly known as Mormonism.

It's a religion: There are currently more than 15 million Mormons around the globe, dedicated to a faith that emphasizes following the example of Jesus Christ. Mormons serve missions, build temples, do genealogy, raise larger-than-average families, and believe those families can be together forever.

It's a subculture: Mormonism has a unique and sometimes controversial history. Some of its early practices have been totally disavowed by the modern church (e.g., polygamy), but others have become more important today than they were when the religion first started in the nineteenth century (e.g., the Word of Wisdom—Mormonism's dietary code that forbids alcohol and coffee). This subculture has its own distinguishing behavior, its own heroes, and its own lingo—all of which can be baffling to outsiders. Even as Mormonism expands internationally, its "home base" subculture in and around Salt Lake City, Utah, sets the tone for the church around the world.

And now, Mormonism is indeed the focus of a wildly popular Broadway musical, *The Book of Mormon*. That show, or perhaps other references to Mormonism in pop culture, may have played a part in your decision to pick up this book. Lots of people are curious about the Church of Jesus Christ of Latter-day Saints, whether they've seen the musical, voted (or not voted) for Mormon political candidates like Mitt Romney, or just wondered why their Mormon neighbors seem so squeaky-clean. Mormonism is everywhere, but reliable information about the religion and its people can be hard to find. Some accounts produced by the LDS Church are glowing propaganda, while some written by outsiders or ex-Mormons are sensationalistic diatribes aimed at discrediting the Mormon faith.

The truth lies somewhere in the middle, which is why you need this book. It joins a growing body of literature about Mormonism that aims to educate you—not to convert (or deconvert) you from what you already believe. A decade ago, I attempted a similar task. Trust me when I say that it's not easy to introduce an entire religion in a single book that is balanced, reasonably comprehensive, and blessedly *short*. And there are very few one-volume introductions that pass muster with flying colors, as this book does.

Mormonism for Beginners assumes you might know a little something about Mormonism but would like to know more, and it teaches you with both humor and intelligence. Stephen Carter is a terrific choice for writing this book. He is a Mormon himself who has all the "insider" credentials you want in an author, but he also possesses a critical eye. As the editor of a magazine about Mormon belief and culture, he has his finger on the pulse of Mormons today. As a novelist and storyteller, he is alive to the beauty and originality of the Mormon story. And as someone who has brought the Book of Mormon to life as a comic series, he understands well how to tell the story of Mormonism with more than just text. In this book, he and artist Jett Atwood—who collaborated together on the *iPlates* comics about the Book of Mormon—blend words and pictures to give you a portrait of Mormonism that is both educational and fun to read.

In other words, *Mormonism For Beginners* introduces the religion and the subculture in an entertaining way. Enjoy!

Jana Riess is a senior columnist for Religion News Service, writing primarily about Mormonism. She is the co-author of Mormonism for Dummies *and* Mormonism and American Politics, *among other books. She holds a PhD in the history of religion in America from Columbia University.*

Introduction

"**M**y first serious girlfriend, when I was 16, was Mormon," said Trey Parker, one of the creators of *South Park* and *The Book of Mormon* musical. "I went to her house for 'family home evening,' and I was like, 'Why aren't you people ignoring each other and watching television?'" Parker's remark encapsulates what many Americans perceive about members of the Church of Jesus Christ of Latter-day Saints: that they are a kind of extended episode of *Ozzie and Harriet* or *Leave It to Beaver*—family values and clean living coming out the wazoo.

But Mormons are certainly more than that. Despite making up only 1.7 percent of the U.S. population (by contrast, Evangelical Christians make up 26 percent), Latter-day Saints are deeply integrated into American life: they're business leaders, national politicians, athletes, pop stars, and— since there are more than 6 million of them in the United States—likely somebody in your neighborhood. About a third of American Mormons live in Utah, with the LDS Church based in Salt Lake City, but the rest make their homes in every corner of the country.

Mormonism is also becoming a noticeable presence worldwide, with more members living outside the United States than inside. Members of the LDS Church make up 40 percent of the population of Samoa, while Argentina, Chile, and Peru have approximately half a million Mormons each. Brazil is home to over 1.2 million Latter-day Saints.

But it wasn't always like this. During the LDS Church's early years

Mormons Through the Ages?

1850s

1880s

1930s

1950s

Donny & Marie

1970s

2000s

in frontier America, Mormons numbered only in the thousands and were often considered strange or even dangerous. After all, they had a new book of scripture, a charismatic prophet, plans to build Zion, and an unusual marriage practice. Considering the antagonism and persecution that dogged early Mormonism, the fact that it has not only survived but actually flourished when so many other 19th-century American religions have dwindled or disappeared is a testament to its vitality.

Even today, with Mormons holding positions of prominence throughout American society and with the LDS Church operating major institutions in business, education, and the media, questions and curiosities persist about them in mainstream society. Some Americans still ask if Mormons practice polygamy. Others have heard of the "holy underwear" and wonder what *that's* all about. Do Mormons really believe that Jesus visited America after his resurrection? Do all young Mormons really take two years off to serve as missionaries? Why does the LDS Church maintain such a vast archive of genealogical information? Are African Americans allowed in the Church? Can women hold the priesthood?

Getting a handle on Mormonism can sometimes be a difficult proposition. Though in many ways it looks like a Protestant denomination, in other ways it is very different. Mormon theology has elements of both monotheism and polytheism. The Church uses not just one but *three* additional books of scripture along with the Bible. And, though the LDS Church has a history of polygamy, it now excommunicates anyone who enters the practice. In other words, Mormonism is a complex, evolving religion.

Beyond all that, as much or more than any other faith practiced in America today, Mormonism is not just a system of religious beliefs but also a way of life, a system of social values, and a tight-knit community. Its precepts establish rules and parameters for everyday living and social interaction, with a history, tradition, and governing authority all its own.

And so, even with the Church's growth and success over the course of nearly two centuries, people in the United States still retain some suspicions about it. In a 2014 Pew Survey, respondents placed Mormons third from the bottom (scoring 48) in how warmly they regarded various religious groups. (Atheists scored 41 and Muslims 40. Jews ranked highest at 63.) So there is still plenty of work to do as far as familiarizing people with Mormonism.

You might say that Mormons are trying to do their part, what with the tens of thousands of missionaries they deploy around the world each year. But some people who are curious about Mormonism may not quite be ready to let those chipper kids through the front door.

And there is also a *lot* to learn about it—so much is different from other Christian churches and faiths.

This book aims to give readers a private introduction to this young, but fascinating, religion and lifestyle: exploring the life of Church founder Joseph Smith, the Book of Mormon, LDS theology, what goes on inside temples, the milestones of a Mormon life, and the controversies with which Church members are wrestling. Read it with an open mind and, as in the case of all For Beginners books, consider it a starting point for deeper exploration. The list of books and websites provided in the Further Reading section is a good place to begin.

One last note: To avoid confusion, it's important to remember that a number of churches trace their theological roots to Joseph Smith, such as Community of Christ, the "Strangites," and the Apostolic United Brethren. Some of them are mentioned in this book, others not. *Mormonism For Beginners* focuses on the "Salt Lake Church"— The Church of Jesus Christ of Latter-day Saints— since it is by far the largest and most influential of the branches.

...I DON'T KNOW MUCH ABOUT THE MORMONS!

part 1

MORMON HISTORY

Brother Joseph

JOSEPH SMITH

Make no mistake. Mormons consider Joseph Smith, the founder of Mormonism, to be the greatest prophet in world history, ranking second only to Jesus Christ. This is an extraordinary claim that raises the question: *Just what is a prophet?*

Some might consider prophets to be serene people whose reputations are ever spotless—people who establish only peace around them, whose every step seems blessed by God. But that was not Joseph Smith. His explosive brand of prophethood broke down social and theological walls, mended millennia-old rifts in human and cultural understanding, and threw itself against the limits of the heart's capacity. Those who interacted with Joseph Smith were inevitably drawn into his intense, frequently overwhelming maelstrom. And in that tempest, they either lost themselves or found themselves. Sometimes both. Joseph's life was a holy storm—both vitalizing and disrupting—whose potency still draws people into its heart almost 200 years after his death. *Smithsonian Magazine* in 2015 ranked Joseph Smith as *the* most influential religious figure in American history.

Early Life

Born on December 23, 1805, Joseph Smith grew up in upstate New York in what was called the "burned-over district," so named for the numerous tent revival meetings that swept through the area. Though his family was religious, they weren't attached to a particular church and often participated in these revivals.

Joseph and his family were also very much into folk magic, which often blended into frontier Christianity. Joseph frequently took nighttime excursions around the forest, leading groups of people with a divining rod or peep stone (also called a seer stone) and performing elaborate rituals in an attempt to detect hidden treasures beneath the ground.

Joseph was also obsessed about which, if any, of the Christian churches in his area possessed the whole truth. His search for that answer leads us to Mormonism's foundational story: the First Vision.

The First Vision

Though the First Vision of 1820 is at the base of Mormonism's conception of itself, Joseph Smith never actually committed the story to paper until 1832, two years after he founded the LDS Church. In that earliest version, he describes his 16-year-old self (though he was actually 14 if the vision took place in 1820) as being disenchanted with the churches he had come into contact with, feeling that that none of them had the truth. He describes going into the forest near his home in the town of Palmyra, praying about the matter, and being visited by the "Lord," whom Smith records as saying, "behold the world lieth in sin at this time and none doeth good no not one they have turned aside from the gospel and keep not my commandments." (Letterbook 1, The Joseph Smith Papers)

In 1835, Smith recounted his vision again to a religious charismatic named Robert Matthews. In this telling, Smith says that he had been merely perplexed by the different denominations (instead of being convinced that they had no truth) and had been inspired by Matthew 7:7 and James 1:5 to seek divine answers. He goes into the woods to pray but, in this account, has difficulty doing so: his tongue swells in his mouth and he becomes frightened by the sound of footsteps behind him. Soon, a "pillar of fire" descends over him, illuminates the forest, and fills him "with joy unspeakable." One "personage" stands in the pillar of fire for a fleeting moment; then another one descends, telling Joseph that his sins are forgiven and testifying of Jesus Christ. Joseph also sees angels. (Journal, 1835–1836, The Joseph Smith Papers)

But the story that eventually became the accepted version among Mormons was written as a part of Joseph Smith's official history in 1838. This narrative is the most detailed. First, it spends a good amount of space describing how the Second Great Awakening—the Protestant revival movement that swept America during the first decades of the 19th century—affected young Joseph. Seeking the true faith, Smith runs across James 1:5, which reads, "If any of you lack wisdom, let him ask of God, that giveth to all men liberally, and upbraideth not; and it shall be given him."

And so, according to the official version of the First Vision, on the "morning of a beautiful, clear day, early in the spring of eighteen hundred and twenty," young Joseph Smith walks into a grove of trees and, for the first time in his life, begins to pray vocally. "I had scarcely done so," he continues, "when

> **immediately I was seized upon by some power which entirely overcame me, and had such an astonishing influence over me as to bind my tongue so that I could not speak. Thick darkness gathered around me, and it seemed to me for a time as if I were doomed to sudden destruction."**

And then he pens the words that have launched a million Mormon missionary lessons:

> [J]ust at this moment of great alarm, I saw a pillar of light exactly over my head, above the brightness of the sun, which descended gradually until it fell upon me. . . . When the light rested upon me I saw two Personages, whose brightness and glory defy all description, standing above me in the air. One of them spake unto me, calling me by name and said, pointing to the other—This is My Beloved Son. Hear Him! (HISTORY 1:16–17)

When Joseph regains possession of himself, he asks the two Personages which church he should he join. As he recounts,

> **I was answered that I must join none of them, for they were all wrong; and the Personage who addressed me said that all their creeds were an abomination in his sight; that those professors were all corrupt. . . .**

A few days later, Joseph recounted his vision to a local preacher, who "treated my communication not only lightly, but with great contempt, saying it was all of the devil. . . ." (History 1:21) Indeed, Joseph said that he suffered a good deal of persecution over the years for talking about his vision. (It seems people didn't react well to being told that their religion is an abomination!)

In 1842, Joseph penned his final version of the story in what came to be called the Wentworth Letter. It's pretty much an abbreviation of the 1838 version, but with the added detail that the

> **"two glorious personages . . . exactly resembled each other in features and likeness," and with a promise from the divine personages that "the fullness of the gospel should at some future time be made known to me."** ("Church History," *Times and Seasons*, 3 (9): 706–10)

These various accounts of the First Vision have caused a great deal of debate between Mormons and their critics. Joseph Smith seems to have told different stories each time, beginning with one heavenly being, then adding another, and then sprinkling in some angels—not to mention failing to describe the demonic attack the first time around. Many theories have been advanced to explain these differences, but there is little doubt of the narrative's potency. It is probably the most-told story in Mormonism.

The Great Apostasy

All of this raises the question, why did God need to visit Joseph Smith and tell him all of the churches are wrong in the first place? Mormons came to explain this as the Great Apostasy.

It was the killing of Jesus's original apostles that led to this falling away: a period of about 1,700 years during which God's priesthood was found nowhere in the Eastern Hemisphere. (It *was* extant in the Americas, but we'll get to that in the section on the Book of Mormon.) Bits and pieces of the truth remained, but not God's authority—the priesthood. As Jesus once said to Peter, "I will give unto thee the keys of the kingdom of heaven: and whatsoever thou shalt bind on earth shall be bound in heaven: and whatsoever thou shalt loose on earth shall be loosed in heaven." (Matthew 16:19) *That's the priesthood.* Mormons

see priesthood authority as essential to acting in God's name. Without it, no matter how well-intentioned one might be, rites such as baptism are not recognized by the heavens.

Compelling reasons why the Great Apostasy lasted such a long time are difficult to find in Mormon discourse. The best you can usually dig up is that God spent a millennium and three-quarters preparing earth to receive the truth again, notably by inspiring Martin Luther to launch the Protestant reformation and by assisting the Founding Fathers of the United States in developing a political environment tolerant of diverse religious views and practices (though not entirely, as we'll see later).

Things didn't start getting back on track until the Second Great Awakening and the evangelical fervor it brought to much of frontier America in the early 19th century. Those who participated in the Second Great Awakening focused on getting as close to original Christianity as possible, stripping away all the traditions that had built up around and obscured the purity of Jesus's gospel. They were called "restorationists" because they wanted to restore Christ's original church.

Joseph Smith's vision was not just a remarkable personal manifestation but a call to restore the very church Jesus himself had established during his brief three-year ministry.

Angelic Visit

After his First Vision in 1820, Smith heard very little from heaven. Then, in 1823, he said he was lying in bed, praying for forgiveness of his sins, when. . .

I discovered a light appearing in my room, which continued to increase until the room was lighter than at noonday, when immediately a personage appeared at my bedside, standing in the air . . . He said there was a book deposited, written upon gold plates, giving an account of the former inhabitants of this continent, and the source from

whence they sprang. He also said that the fulness of the everlasting Gospel was contained in it, as delivered by the Savior to the ancient inhabitants. . . . While he was conversing with me about the plates, the vision was opened to my mind that I could see the place where the plates were deposited. (History 1:30–42)

It was an amazing vision by anyone's standards, but the night was still young! As it turned out, the messenger reappeared to Joseph two more times that evening.

So Joseph didn't get any sleep that night. In fact, he was so exhausted the next morning that he was unable to do his chores. His father sent him back to the house, but when Joseph tried to cross the fence, he fell and lost consciousness. A voice awoke him, and he looked up to see the same messenger from the night before, delivering the same message. This time, the messenger told Joseph to go dig up the gold plates.

> **I left the field, and went to the place where the messenger had told me the plates were deposited; and owing to the distinctness of the vision which I had had concerning it, I knew the place the instant that I arrived there.** (HISTORY 1:50)

Smith said he did a little digging, used a branch as a lever to dislodge a large stone, and found a stone box beneath it.

> **I looked in, and there indeed did I behold the plates, the Urim and Thummim, and the breastplate, as stated by the messenger. . . .**
>
> **I made an attempt to take them out, but was forbidden by the messenger, and was again informed that the time for bringing them forth had not yet arrived, neither would it, until four years from that time; but he told me that I should come to that place precisely in one year from that time, and that he would there meet with me, and that I should continue to do so until the time should come for obtaining the plates.** (HISTORY 1:52–53)

And that is just what Joseph says he did, meeting the angel annually for the next four years to receive instruction. During that last meeting, the angel finally allowed him to take the gold plates and its translators.

BOOK OF MORMON
TRANSLATION

Most images you will see of Joseph Smith translating the golden plates, producing the Book of Mormon, will show him sitting at a table, bent over the plates like a monk—the finger of one hand resting on one thin golden sheet, his other hand pressed to his brow. On the other side of the table will sit a scribe, diligently taking down Joseph's words.

But there are many accounts of how Smith translated the plates. His first wife, Emma Hale Smith, said that he translated some of the first 116 pages of the Book of Mormon by putting on the breastplate he found with the plates and peering through the Urim and Thummim—a pair of transparent stones that took their designation from a phrase in the Hebrew Bible often translated as "revelation and truth"—which were attached to the breastplate with silver bows.

According to most testimonies of the translation process, Joseph spent the majority of his time peering at a seer stone inside his hat, especially a chocolate-colored stone that he had found while digging a well many years before. According to some second-hand accounts, given years after the fact, Joseph said that words would appear as if on a piece of lighted parchment over the stone until he conveyed them to the scribe, after which they would disappear—as if the stone were a cell phone receiving heavenly text messages.

The Golden Plates

The golden plates were actually hidden from view for much of the time Joseph was translating the Book of Mormon. A few people said that they had seen the plates, such as the "Three Witnesses" who testify at the beginning of the Book of Mormon that an angel showed them the plates, and the "Eight Witnesses" who say that Joseph Smith let them handle the plates, "and we also saw the engravings thereon, all of which has the appearance of ancient work, and of curious workmanship." Emma Smith said that she often handled the plates while they were wrapped in a cloth, moving them from place to place as she did household chores, but that she never actually unwrapped them.

Most of the physical descriptions of the golden plates portray them as a kind of three-ring binder: rectangular in shape (measuring about 7 inches wide and 8 inches long); each page a little thinner than a tin plate; inscribed with "reformed Egyptian" characters; bound together with three D-shaped rings; and weighing between 30 and 60 pounds.

The Lost 116 Pages

Joseph soon realized that translating golden plates wasn't putting food on the table, and Emma was ready to give birth to their first child. Fortunately, a well-to-do man named Martin Harris became a kind of patron to Joseph. But Harris's wife wasn't too hot on the young prophet or her husband's willingness to give him their money. She demanded to see what Joseph was doing, and Martin asked Joseph to let him show her the first 116 pages (which had been written out by hand but not yet copied), hoping they would change her heart. Against his better judgment, Joseph allowed Martin to take the pages.

Shortly thereafter, Joseph and Emma's first child was stillborn.

Then, still grief-stricken, Joseph received news that the 116 pages had disappeared and that God was *mad* about it. In fact, a whole section of the Doctrine and Covenants (the Mormon scripture containing God's revelations to Joseph Smith) is dedicated to God raking Joseph over the coals for the loss of the pages and suspending his ability to translate.

Priesthood Restored

The translation began again after a few months, continuing for another year and a half. During that time, Joseph and his scribe, Oliver Cowdery, said they were visited by a resurrected John the Baptist who gave them the Aaronic Priesthood. Then the resurrected Peter, James, and John—Jesus's apostles—bestowed the Melchizedek Priesthood upon them. This event is one of the cornerstones of Mormonism's claim to truthfulness. If God's priesthood had disappeared from the earth with the death of Jesus's apostles, now the apostles came back to restore it. Every male in the Mormon Church who receives the Aaronic or Melchizedek Priesthood can trace his priestly "lineage" back to this event.

Book of Mormon Published

The story of the golden plates spread through upstate New York and brought Smith much attention, both positive and negative. Some people tried to steal the plates, others refused to believe they existed, and still other were so captivated by the discovery and translation process that they became Smith's followers.

WAIT! ...THIS READS LIKE A NOVEL! WHERE ARE THE VERSES?

In June 1829, Joseph applied for a copyright for the Book of Mormon, but he didn't have the money to print it. So he sent some followers off to Canada to sell the Canadian copyright, but that didn't work out either. Once again, Martin Harris had to come to the rescue, pledging his farm against the cost of printing the first 5,000 copies. A year later, he had to auction off 151 acres to cover the bill.

Church Founded

On April 6, 1830, in Fayette, New York, 24-year-old Joseph Smith organized what he called "the Church of Jesus Christ." Unfortunately, that name was already taken—many times over, in fact—which is why it eventually morphed into the Church of Jesus Christ of Latter-day Saints. Approximately 60 believers showed up for the founding event, 20 of them having traveled 100 miles to attend.

ON THE ROAD

Six months after the Church was organized, four missionaries were dispatched to preach to Native Americans on the western border of Missouri. Though the missionaries had some success there, they hit the real jackpot when they stopped near Kirtland, Ohio, where one of the missionaries visited a former teacher and minister. The minister's name was Sidney Rigdon, then leading a Baptist-influenced congregation. Rigdon invited the missionaries to preach to his flock. He and many of his followers were so affected by the missionaries, and so enthralled by the Book of Mormon, that they agreed to be baptized into the Church. By the time the missionaries were finished, there were more Mormons in Ohio than there were in New York.

In December 1830, Rigdon traveled to New York to meet Joseph Smith and was almost immediately called as a scribe to Smith for his "inspired translation" of the Bible. Doubtless due to the many conversations that transpired between the two men, and the rising persecution of Mormons in New York, Kirtland started to sound like a great place to transplant the budding church. Just after New Year's in 1831, Smith dictated a revelation commanding the

NEW YORK OHIO

CHURCH GROWTH

Saints (members of the Church) to move, promising "greater riches, even a land of promise, a land flowing with milk and honey, upon which there shall be no curse when the Lord cometh." (D&C 38:18)

After reaching Kirtland, Smith faced the problem of taking care of all the new arrivals. Through another revelation, he outlined the "law of consecration," which required Saints to deed all their property to the Church's bishop, who would then divvy up the property among Church members according to their needs. Each family was given free rein to manage the property until the end of the year, when they were mandated to give any surplus that was beyond their needs back to the bishop so that it could be bequeathed to the newest batch of arrivals. The law focused on creating an egalitarian society. In fact, in one of Smith's revelations, God says in no uncertain terms, "it is not given that one man should possess that which is above another, wherefore the world lieth in sin." (D&C 49:20)

Revelations

About those revelations: there were a lot of them in these years. During the course of his life, Joseph Smith received over 170 revelations. Many but not all of them are canonized in the Doctrine and Covenants. Of these revelations, nearly 150 were received in New York and Kirtland. Most were for individual members called into church service. But the wisdom and insights of the revelations led Smith to publish them, first under the title *Book of Commandments* in 1833, and then as the *Doctrine and Covenants* in 1835.

Finding Zion

When one of the biggest landowners in Kirtland went back on his contract and kicked the Mormon settlers off his land, Smith, following yet another revelation, sent this group on to Missouri to establish a new colony. He soon followed them with a group of freshly minted Church leaders.

Upon their arrival, Smith received a revelation telling him that this area, Jackson County, Missouri, would be where the New Jerusalem, or Zion, would be built. In fact, it was revealed that this was also the place where Jesus would launch the Second Coming.

Excited to be a part of the prophecy's fulfillment, Mormons flocked into Jackson County. By the middle of 1833, more than 1,200 Church members had settled there, and they made no secret of their intentions: Zion's city plans were already on paper! This concerned the earlier white settlers and deepened the cultural divide between the Yankee Mormons and Southern Missourians. Even if they were skeptical that Jesus would choose Missouri for his grand return, they could see that the Mormons could easily take control of political affairs if they voted as a bloc. The Mormons also tended to trade only with each other, depressing the local economy. Add to that the possibility that Mormons would push Missouri toward being an abolitionist state—another blow to the economy—and you can see why general sentiment toward the Mormons turned sour.

Conflicts

So sour, in fact, that many Mormon settlements were raided, houses were torn down, and families were cast into the elements. Hundreds of Church members became refugees; some died from exposure or violence. And then things got worse. After bearing a number of attacks without retaliation, the Mormons finally defended themselves in a conflict that developed near the Big Blue River in the fall of 1833. Two Missourians and one Mormon were killed in an exchange of fire.

The conflict continued for months. Mormon leader Lyman Wight reported as follows:

> **I saw one hundred and ninety women and children driven thirty miles across the prairie, with three decrepit men only in their company, in the month of November, the ground thinly crusted with sleet; and I could easily follow on their trail by the blood that flowed from their lacerated feet on the stubble of the burnt prairie!** *(HC 3:439)*

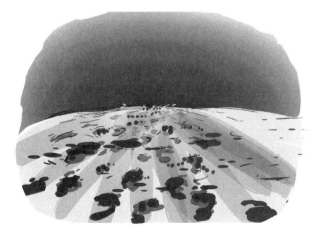

ZION'S CAMP

J oseph Smith, stationed in Kirtland, Ohio, received a revelation in December 1833 directing him to gather together a group charged with "redeeming Zion"—in other words, helping the Mormons in Jackson County reclaim their property, by force if necessary. Joseph would lead the party, called the Camp of Israel, himself. The story of Zion's Camp, as it came to be known, is a microcosm of what made Joseph Smith such a powerful and controversial figure.

It took a lot of work on the part of many missionaries to gather enough volunteers to make the trip worthwhile. But when the departure date finally arrived in early May, only 20 people showed up. Joseph sent them ahead and went about scaring up the rest. The Mormons in Kirtland, struggling to build their first temple, weren't terribly well off to begin with. This trip, as righteous and essential as it seemed, took husbands away from their families and strained already scant resources. Many women and children were left to fend for themselves during the months the Camp was away.

A 1,000-mile Journey

The journey was rarely pleas-ant for the 207 men, 11 women and 11 children who took part. Sometimes they marched 35 miles a day, usually on an empty or upset stomach.

...HOW LONG BEFORE McDONALDS IS INVENTED?

According to some accounts, the marchers had to survive on "sour bread," rancid butter, and "stinking ham." Some were so desperate with thirst that they drank strained swamp water.

But Joseph Smith was in top prophetic form during the journey, perceiving in the land sacred histories and evidences of the divine. One day, the travelers came across a large mound of earth. "On the top of the mound" wrote Joseph, were stones which presented the appearance of three altars having been erected one above the other, accord-ing to the ancient order; and the remains of bones were strewn over the surface of the ground." (HC 2:79) A few men dug in the mound and uncovered a human skeleton with an arrowhead lodged between its ribs. Smith wrote,

> [T]he visions of the past being opened to my under-standing by the Spirit of the Almighty, I discov-ered that the person whose skeleton was before us was a white Lamanite [one of the peoples described in the Book of Mormon], a large, thick-set man, and a man of God. His name was Zelph. He was a warrior and chieftain under the great prophet Onandagus, who was known from the Hill Cumorah, or eastern sea to the Rocky mountains. *(HC 2:80)*

Here the prophet was unfolding Book of Mormon history right before his companions' eyes. It was this stunning ability to make the world around his followers come alive that endeared Smith to so many of them. Other Judeo-Christian believers heard Biblical tales about the Holy Land 6,000 miles away, a place they would never see, full of relics they would never touch—after all, during the 1830s, the Holy Land was not enshrined in photographs and certainly not yet depicted on celluloid. But the men and women of Zion's Camp were, in Joseph's own words in a letter to his wife Emma, "wandering over the plains of the Nephites, recounting occasionally the history of the Book of Mormon, roving over the mounds of that once beloved people of the Lord, picking up their skulls & their bones, as a proof of its divine authenticity."

Joseph also introduced a surprising strain of pacifism into this militaristic camp. While setting up tents, Joseph and a few others came across three rattlesnakes, which the men were planning to kill. But, according to his own account, Smith declared,

> **Let them alone—don't hurt them! How will the serpent ever lose his venom, while the servants of God possess the same disposition, and continue to make war upon it? . . . when men lose their vicious dispositions and cease to destroy the animal race, the lion and the lamb can dwell together, and the sucking child can play with the serpent in safety.** (HC 2:71)

Joseph's journal records a number of other snake encounters during the journey that ended peacefully, except for the time Martin Harris deliberately annoyed one, trying to show how his faith would protect him from its bite. His faith apparently wasn't strong enough.

Close Calls

The camp experienced many close calls during the journey. In one incident, Smith recorded that 15 Missourians started out to gather a mob to destroy Zion's Camp, but while they were crossing a river "an angel of God saw fit to sink the boat about the middle of the river." Many of the men drowned. One "floated down the river some four or five miles, and lodged upon a pile of drift wood, where the eagles, buzzards, ravens, crows, and wild animals ate his flesh from his bones . . . and left him a horrible example of God's vengeance." (HC 2:100)

The climax of the journey occurred when a mob of about 200 men started to cross a river in order to destroy the Mormon militia. About 40 of them made it to shore, but then a "squall" hit, preventing anyone else from crossing. Wrote Smith,

The storm was tremendous, wind and rain, hail and thunder met them in great wrath. . . . it seemed as if the mandate of vengeance had gone forth from the God of battles, to protect His servants from the destruction of their enemies, for the hail fell on them and not on us, and we suffered no harm . . . while our enemies had holes made in their hats, and otherwise received damage, even the breaking of their rifle stocks, and the fleeing of their horses through fear and pain. . . . They reported that one of their men was killed by lightning, and that another had his hand torn off by his horse drawing his hand between the logs of a corn crib while he was holding him on the inside. (HC 2:105)

GOD HAS SAVED US!

The Epidemic

But only a day or two after being miraculously preserved, the party was suddenly laid flat by an outbreak of cholera. According to Smith's diary, he had warned the camp a few days earlier that, because of their disobedience, "God had decreed that sickness should come upon the camp, and if they did not repent and humble themselves before God they should die like sheep with the rot; that I was sorry, but could not help it." (HC 2:106).

Fourteen people died of cholera in just a couple of days. Even Joseph was afflicted "The moment I attempted to rebuke the disease I was attacked and had I not desisted in my attempt to save the life of a brother, I would have sacrificed my own." (HC 2:114)

During the epidemic, Joseph received a revelation: Zion's Camp had failed because of the unfaithfulness of the Mormons—specifically because they "do not impart of their substance as becometh saints, to the poor and afflicted among them . . ." (D&C 105:3) "Therefore it is expedient in me that mine Elders should wait for a little season, for the redemption of Zion." (D&C 105:13) Almost 200 years after Zion's Camp, that redemption still has not occurred. Apparently, Mormons have not yet learned how to impart of their substance to the poor and afflicted.

The End of Zion's Camp

With this revelation, Joseph disbanded Zion's Camp in July 1834 and prepared the company to make the return trip to Kirtland, much to the outrage of many of its members; some left Mormonism altogether. But the fascinating thing is how *few* people left the faith over Zion's Camp, and, in fact, how many of Mormonism's future leaders were a part of this apparently epic failure. Months of time and tremendous resources had been poured into the venture, 14 people had died, and no progress had been made

in restoring Mormons to their property in Jackson County, but Joseph managed to use the harrowing expedition to invest his followers even more deeply in himself and the Mormon faith.

In one of his revelations, Joseph was called a seer (D&C 21:1). Indeed, to his followers, the world around him seemed brimming with divine potential. Great past occurrences could manifest themselves, angels could be detected, a storm could be full of God. With Joseph's eye upon it, eternity could indeed dwell in a grain of sand, or a rattlesnake, or a bedraggled human being, still weak from cholera, facing a 1,000-mile journey home.

KIRTLAND

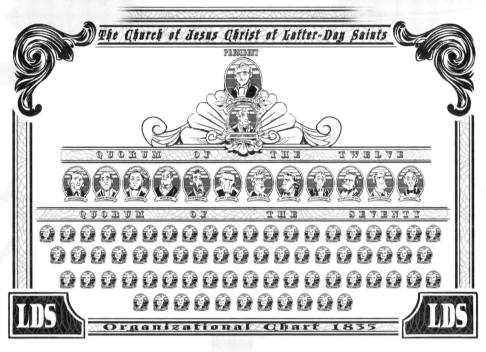

The Church of Jesus Christ of Latter-Day Saints

PRESIDENT

QUORUM OF THE TWELVE

QUORUM OF THE SEVENTY

LDS — LDS

Organizational Chart 1835

Back in Kirtland, the Church began to take on its organizational shape. Smith put together the First Presidency (the three men who led the Church), the Council of Twelve Apostles (one step down from the First Presidency), and a few local offices like high councilor, stake president, and bishop.

Organization was on Smith's mind because Kirtland was growing like crazy, many new Mormons arriving penniless. Smith tried to remedy the problem through the United Order, but with limited success. Nevertheless, in spring 1833, following a directive from God in another revelation to their prophet, the Saints of Kirtland started building a temple. The women made clothing for the temple builders and the men "tithed" their time, spending one day in every ten constructing the temple.

Yet peace remained elusive. The persecutions that had followed the

Mormons from New York to Kirtland and from Kirtland to Missouri, continued to dog them for the same reasons: controversial beliefs, a tendency toward economic and cultural insularity, voting as a bloc, and persistent poverty. The temple project had to be guarded at all times from anti-Mormon vandals.

Meanwhile, Smith was busily at work on new scripture. He continued his "inspired translation" of the Bible, adding much to Genesis and Matthew. He also bought some mummies and their accompanying papyrus, which he said contained some of Abraham's writings. Later, in Nauvoo, Illinois, he translated these documents as the Book of Abraham. That work adds some interesting backstory to Abraham's life, such as an account of being saved by an angel from a priest's sacri-

ficial knife (adding a layer of irony to Abraham's later attempt at sacrificing Isaac), and a story about the 'war in heaven" that has affected Mormonism to the present day.

Smith also continued to receive revelations on a variety of subjects, such as how many degrees of heaven there are (three), health codes (no coffee, tea, alcohol, tobacco, or meat in excess), and plural marriage (to be discussed later in this section).

After three years of construction, the Kirtland Temple was dedicated on March 27, 1836. The dedication was much like the Day

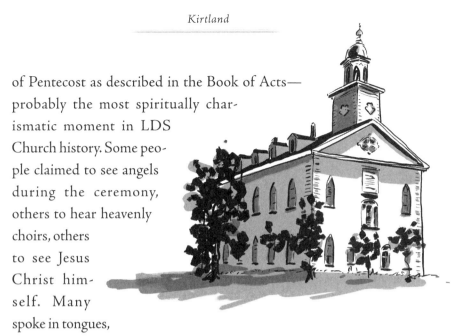

of Pentecost as described in the Book of Acts—probably the most spiritually charismatic moment in LDS Church history. Some people claimed to see angels during the ceremony, others to hear heavenly choirs, others to see Jesus Christ himself. Many spoke in tongues, saw visions, and prophesied. In the days after the dedication, Joseph Smith and Oliver Cowdery said they were visited in the temple by Jesus Christ, Elijah, Elias, and Moses.

But the temple had demanded a steep economic price from the community, and the Mormons were having a difficult time getting credit from the local banks. So Kirtland tried to gain a charter from Ohio to organize its own bank, the Kirtland Safety Society. This was back when banks issued their own currency notes, and the Church had already bought printing plates for that purpose. But the Ohio legislature granted only one bank charter that year, and it wasn't to the Mormons.

Never ones to waste anything, the Church proceeded to print bills with the prefix "anti" before "bank" and the suffix "ing" after it, thereby declaring the "Kirtland Safety Society Anti-Banking Company"—a quasi-bank. This wasn't quite as shifty as it sounds. There was no national currency in the 1830s, and banks popped up all over the country after Andrew Jackson dissolved the Second National Bank. Even businesses issued their own currency and bank notes.

But the quasi-bank in Kirtland issued too many bills, and most of the funds backing the bills were tied up in land. The onset of the

Panic of 1837 sent everyone running to cash their notes, and the bank closed down before the year was out.

A lot of people lost a lot of money, and they were very angry about it. They were so angry in fact, that, according to an informant, an assassination attempt was being planned on Smith. So the Mormon prophet scooted out of Kirtland as fast as he could go, heading for Missouri. The rest of the Saints (at least the ones that hadn't apostatized over the failing bank) followed shortly thereafter, leaving their homes and most of their possessions to be snatched up by waiting neighbors.

MISSOURI

Missouri was not much better than Kirtland. Its main attraction was that people weren't actively trying to kill Smith at the moment.

Life had not become any easier for the Missouri Mormons since the failed Zion's Camp expedition. Though they tried every legal means possible, appealing to the governor and even President Andrew Jackson, they never got back their land in Jackson County. They had taken temporary refuge in Clay County, whose citizens were accommodating at first. Once again, however, the Mormons started to outnumber the original settlers and began talking about how they were going to take things over. So the residents of Clay County encouraged them to look for another place to settle.

And look they did. In fact, they convinced a state legislator to create an entire county (Caldwell County) just for the Mormons, complete with a three-mile buffer zone between them and the next county. In 1836, they started to build a settlement called Far West, named for its location within the county, and it looked as if they were finally going to get some peace.

But Mormon leaders began to "cleanse" the Church of dissenters, who vented their grievances to people in the surrounding counties,

riling them up once again. Meanwhile, Sidney Rigdon delivered a speech that sounded like a declaration of war against apostates and outsiders, enflaming the surrounding citizenry even more.

Considering the circumstances, Mormons had been a peaceable people until that time, taking their persecution with only occasional retaliation. But now that time was over. Frequent acts of violence against or perpetrated by Mormons destroyed the peace all over Caldwell and Daviess counties: brawls broke out, houses were burned, looting committed, women raped, crops destroyed, families expelled into the elements. All the while, rumors fanned the flames of paranoia. This assemblage of clashes became known as the Mormon War.

News of the conflict reached the ears of Missouri's governor, Lilburn Boggs, who became so convinced of the Mormons' antagonism that he issued the infamous Extermination Order of October 1838. "The Mormons must be treated as enemies," he wrote, "and *must be exterminated* or driven from the state, if necessary for the public good. Their outrages are beyond all description." (HC 3:175)

A carte blanche for vigilantism, Boggs's executive order led to the Haun's Mill Massacre at the end of the month, in which 17 Mormons, including women and children, were murdered by a band of 240 men. Simultaneously, 2,000 state troops laid siege on Far West, not letting up until a number of Church leaders, including Joseph Smith, were taken into custody. Their lives were repeatedly in danger, and they ended up spending four winter months in an unheated jail basement before being allowed to escape during a transfer. The Mormon faithful were given no alternative but to leave Missouri, and they did so destitute.

Governor Boggs' extermination order was not rescinded until 1976. While Mormons still believe that Zion will eventually be established in Missouri, it is also the state most drenched with Mormon blood. For decades after, Mormons who had been alive during the Missouri period never bothered to conceal their con-tempt for the state.

The Mormons must be treated as enemies!

NAUVOO

That said, the death toll in Illinois quickly outstripped the Mormon murders in Missouri. Illinois residents welcomed about 9,000 embattled Saints in early 1839, hoping that the industrious Mormons would help the state's flagging economy. The newcomers settled in a swampy area on the Mississippi River in west-central Illinois, using credit to buy the land (a debt that was never settled). But the area was infested by malaria-carrying mosquitoes, and soon just about everyone was ill. Many stories of miraculous healings sprang from this time, but many deaths occurred as well.

Responding to a letter from Smith, however, thousands of Mormons continued pouring into the region, which was soon named Nauvoo. They built the city and its surrounding area very rapidly until it actually rivaled Chicago in population. This was possible partially because Nauvoo was granted a liberal charter that allowed it to assemble its own militia of up to 5,000 soldiers and to elect its own judges and juries. With the violence of Missouri fresh in the minds of Mormon settlers, the idea of having so much control over their own legal and civil affairs—not to mention a robust army—made the future look bright.

Despite the constant shadow of disease and death, the three years the Saints spent in Nauvoo before Joseph Smith's death are remembered as golden ones. With the city growing rapidly, construction began on a 50,000-square-foot temple. Much of Mormonism's unique theology—such as baptism for the dead and the temple endowment— was developed during this time. Smith also devised Mormon metaphysics, which, as it turns out, is actually physics. "There is no such thing as immaterial matter," he wrote. "All spirit is matter, but it is

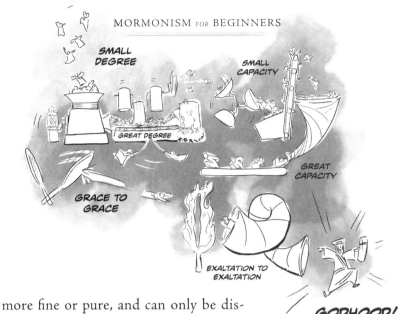

SMALL DEGREE

SMALL CAPACITY

GREAT DEGREE

GREAT CAPACITY

GRACE TO GRACE

EXALTATION TO EXALTATION

GODHOOD!

more fine or pure, and can only be discerned by purer eyes . . ." (D&C 131: 7–8) Smith pushed the idea so far as to say that God "The Father has a body of flesh and bones as tangible as man's; the Son also . . ." (D&C 130:22)

All of which brought Mormon theology to perhaps its most revolutionary doctrine: the idea that human beings are actually gods in embryo. In the famous King Follett Discourse of April 1844, Smith declared,

> **God himself was once as we are now, and is an exalted man, and sits enthroned in yonder heavens! ... [Y]ou have got to learn how to be gods yourselves ... by going from one small degree to another, and from a small capacity to a great one; from grace to grace, from exaltation to exaltation, until you attain to the resurrection of the dead, and are able to dwell in everlasting burnings.**
> (HC 6:302–17)

This doctrine implies that there are actually many gods, and that there will be even more in the future. Some of them will be us.

POLYGAMY AND MARTYRDOM

In many ways, it's not surprising that Mormonism became involved with polygamy (or, more specifically, polygyny—a marital unit consisting of one male and multiple females). Hundreds of new Christian denominations were springing up all over the United States in the early to mid-1800s, and many of them were engaging in social experiments—from the Shakers with their celibate

the utopian american marriage dance

Oneida

Shakers

Mormons

communities, to the Oneida Community with its "complex marriage" system. It's what new religions were doing.

According to his accounts, while Smith was working on his "inspired translation" of the Bible, he came across the story of Sarah giving Hagar to Abraham so that Abraham could have offspring. It seemed to Smith that polygamy was an essential part of an earlier dispensation of the gospel, and he felt called by God to restore *all* things, including this particular form of marriage.

The revelation Smith received reads in part as follows:

> [I]f any man espouse a virgin, and desire to espouse another, and the first give her consent, and if he espouse the second, and they are virgins, and have vowed to no other man, then is he justified; he cannot commit adultery for they are given unto him . . . And if he have ten virgins given unto him by this law, he cannot commit adultery.
>
> (D&C 132:61–62)

Why are multiple wives even needed? The revelation says that the women "are given unto him to multiply and replenish the earth . . . that they may bear the souls of men."

Smith had an innovative view of pre-mortal and post-mortal lives and how they influence earth life. He saw the human race as a big family that must be bound together in order to return to God. No person is whole if he or she is not connected to the rest of humanity through the power of the priesthood. Along with temple work, polygamy was seen as a concrete way of knitting together the human family. Whatever Smith's intentions when he instituted the practice of polygamy, there is no doubt that he inflicted much heartbreak among his family and followers,

all of whom were raised to value monogamy. Indeed, an early chapter of the Book
of Mormon (Jacob 2) condemns polygamy (though,
on close reading, it does make room for the system in particular circumstances). Smith's secret practice of polygamy—he married several dozen wives from the mid-1830s through 1844—played a large
part in rupturing his relationship with his first wife, Emma, when she
found out. From a monogamous point of view, his actions looked like
philandering under the guise of religion.

Smith knew that if word got out about this new practice, he would
likely be strung up. So he introduced it to his inner circle little by little and eventually convinced most of them that it was a heavenly principle. Reading accounts from those days, one can often detect both
great excitement and great anxiety from the "early adopters." To take
part in the restoration of an ancient gospel principle was exhilarating, but its price was the relinquishment of foundational elements of
their emotional and spiritual lives.

In a close-knit community like Nauvoo, rumors were inevitable and
details of Smith's polygamous doings soon slipped out. William Law,
once one of Smith's closest confidants, left the Church over polygamy and started a newspaper called the *Nauvoo Expositor* in June
1844. He published exactly one issue, carrying lengthy stories about
the LDS leadership's clandestine marriage practices, some want ads,
and two poems.

Smith and the Nauvoo city council declared the newspaper a public
menace (not because of the poetry!) and ordered the press destroyed.
Smith came under immediate fire from Thomas Ford, the governor
of Illinois, who insisted that the Mormon leader give himself up for
arrest. After some negotiation, Smith agreed to meet with Ford in the
city of Carthage, not far from Nauvoo. On June 27, however, a mob
attacked the Carthage jail in which Smith and his brother Hyrum
were being held and shot them both dead.

FORGING THE
MORMON
CHARACTER

I f the Mormon mythos was created while Joseph
Smith was alive, the Mormon character was forged during
Brigham Young's presidency.

After the death of Joseph and Hyrum, no one was sure who should
take up the Church's leadership. A few people stepped forward to
make a claim, including Sidney Rigdon, one of Smith's former counselors. Some wanted the prophet's son, Joseph Smith III, to take over.
But at a mass meeting of the faithful, Brigham Young, then in his
mid-forties, won the most hearts by reminding those in attendance of
Smith's revelation that the Quorum of Twelve Apostles—a governing
body he had organized—"was equal in authority and power" to the
presidency. As head of the Quorum of Twelve, Young was ordained
to fill Smith's shoes in December 1847.

He served in a completely different style. While Smith ran the
church mostly through sheer force of charisma and personal mag-
netism, Brigham Young was an organizational powerhouse. He had
proven himself many times through the years, leading the twelve apostles on a stunningly successful mission to Great Britain and keeping
the Mormons together during their expulsion from Missouri.

The death of Joseph Smith allayed much of the animosity that
had built up against the Mormons, providing a measure of respite for
the next two years. But resentment began to be felt once again, and

Church members knew they would need to leave Nauvoo soon. And this time they weren't going to piddle around. Instead of traveling to the next state over, they decided to break clear of the United States entirely and settle in a place where they could run their own affairs, religious and governmental.

OTHER GROUPS

Not all of the Mormon faithful followed Brigham Young, however. A few short-lived groups sprang up almost immediately. David Whitmer, an original "witness" of the Book of Mormon, started a church of his own. Sidney Rigdon led a small group for a little while, out of which William Bickerton established a rival organization—called The Church of Jesus Christ—that still exists today; it claims about 20,000 members worldwide. (Rock star Alice Cooper was active in the Bickertonite Church as a boy.)

MAIN BRANCHES OF THE LATTER DAY SAINT MOVEMENT

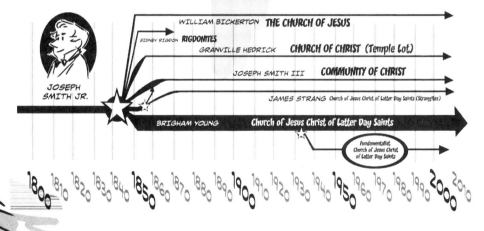

James Strang, who had led a large group of Mormons to colonize Michigan before Joseph Smith's death, founded another offshoot church, claiming to have been visited by angels at the moment of the prophet's passing. The Strangites were the largest Mormon faction aside from to the Brighamites (those who followed Brigham Young and the twelve apostles), but it diminished quickly after Strang was killed in 1856 and the community forcibly broken up by irate neighbors. Adherents to Strang still number in the hundreds today.

Joseph Smith III, the eldest son of the Mormon founder, launched the Reorganized Church of Jesus Christ of Latter Day Saints in 1850

(RLDS, renamed the Community of Christ in 2001). For a long time, the RLDS Church denied that Joseph Smith had started plural marriage and insisted that he never practiced it. Today, with an estimated membership of about a quarter million, the Community of Christ has a more progressive bent than the Church of Jesus Christ of Latter-day Saints, ordaining women to the priesthood in 1984 and allowing same-sex marriage in 2012–2013. The church's headquarters are located at a temple in Independence, Missouri, and it also owns the historic (1836) Kirtland Temple.

In 1863, Granville Hedrick gathered together a disparate group of Mormons and started a church that became known as the Temple Lot group because, for more than 150 years, it has owned the site in Independence, Missouri, that Joseph Smith dedicated for the temple. Today the Hendrickite denomination claims more than 7,000 members worldwide.

CROSSING THE AMERICAN PLAINS

Those who followed Brigham Young began to prepare for migration, but Mormon plans never seemed to work out perfectly. Most Latter-day Saints found themselves driven from Nauvoo by increased mob violence during the winter of 1845–46. The epic journey that followed has left an indelible mark on the Mormon consciousness.

The task of transplanting the community of Mormons across the American plains in the bitter cold, the scorching sun, and all the difficulties of frontier life, is truly mind blowing. This wasn't a simple wagon train, and it wasn't a single crossing. Rather, it was a meticulously prepared, relentlessly organized, several-year migration that eventually brought tens of thousands of Mormons to Salt Lake Valley. But it had a very inauspicious beginning.

At first, Church leaders were hoping to get an advance party settled in the Great Basin by the end of the summer so it could get some crops planted. But the weather did not cooperate. Although a deep freeze allowed most of the Mormons to exit Nauvoo on an iced-over Mississippi River, it also made camping miserable and sometimes fatal. A group of about 1,000 faithful huddled just a few miles outside Nauvoo for nearly a month before travel was

ARE WE THERE YET?!

possible again. Then came an uncharacteristically wet spring, which mired their wagons in mud. By the time four months had passed, the advance party had covered only 300 miles in Iowa; it still had at least 1,000 miles to go. The Saints weren't going to make it in 1846, and Brigham Young knew it. So he set to work doing what he did best: organizing.

Parties of Mormons with varying degrees of discipline were straggled out across 100 miles or so. Young and other leaders traveled back through all of them, regimenting the pioneers into groups of 100, 50, or even 10, each with an assigned leader that reported to the next leader up. Then they started building way stations along the route where companies of Saints could stop to resupply or wait out a winter. At one time or another, these stopping points had populations numbering in the thousands. Young instructed the advance parties to plant crops along the route so that food would be available to those who came after. The Mormons even established a section of their own westward trail along the north side of the Platte River (rather than on the south side, where the Oregon Trail ran) so as not to compete with other migrants for resources.

While the migration was getting underway, some Mormons stayed behind in Nauvoo to finish the temple. In April 1846, a few Church leaders stole back into town and dedicated the building before getting back to their wagon trains. The Saints were so desperate for money, having received little to nothing for their Nauvoo properties, that they actually tried to lease the temple to the Catholic Church and then sell it outright, but no one was buying.

When the last of the Mormon faithful were finally forced out of Nauvoo that summer (at cannon point), the temple was gutted by arsonists.

Unexpected financial help came along when representatives of the U.S. army showed up and asked for 500 men to enlist to fight in the Mexican–American War. At first the Saints refused outright. They had received nothing but neglect from the federal government and weren't feeling particularly for-giving. But Brigham Young knew that the enlisted men would come back with both pay and experience. He man-aged to round up all the required men and launched them on what was probably the lon-gest infantry march in American history: nearly

2,000 miles from Council Bluffs, Iowa, to San Diego, California.

On April 16, 1847, the advance frontier party, called the Pioneer Company, complete with 143 men, three women, two children, at least three black slaves, a slew of wagons, supplies, livestock, and even a boat, started toward Salt Lake Valley. But it wasn't just a journey; it was a preparation for the many Mormons that would follow them. The group brought along barometers, thermometers, and other instru-ments, even building a primitive odometer on the trail—all so they could bring back a detailed report of what succeeding parties could expect.

The company made good time, crossing through Nebraska and then Wyoming. Things slowed down a little when Brigham Young became deathly ill with "Rocky Mountain fever," but the party arrived

intact in Salt Lake Valley between July 21 and 24, 1847. Looking out across the land, Young declared, "It is enough. This is the right place." Then, as some wry historians put it, "they dedicated the land to the Lord, prayed for rain, and built a dam for irrigation in case the rain failed to come." (Leonard Arrington and Davis Bitton in *The Mormon Experience*) The Mormon mindset in a nutshell.

The advance party spent about a month laying out plans for the city and planting crops. Then they took a well-deserved rest by heading straight back to Iowa. On the way, they met the next party of 1,500 Mormons heading west.

The preparations along the trail made crossing the plains much easier for the tens of thousands of Saints who made that journey over the next decades. But getting to Salt Lake Valley was still no walk in the park. Thousands of Mormons died en route, whether from exposure, disease, malnutrition, wildlife attack, or—most commonly—accident. It was a rare family that could make the long journey without losing one or more of its loved ones along the way. Many modern-day Mormons who have pioneer ancestry tell and retell the stories of family hardship, remembering those who were lost and celebrating the ones who survived.

A song by early Church leader William Clayton quickly became an anthem to the unremitting sacrifice that attended the Mormon experience during this period.

Come, come, ye Saints, no toil or labor fear;
But with joy wend your way.
Though hard to you this journey may appear,
Grace shall be as your day...

And should we die before our journey's through,
Happy day! All is well!
We then are free from toil and sorry too;
With the just we shall dwell!

But if our lives are spared again
To see the Saints their rest obtain,
O how we'll make this chorus swell—
All is well! All is well!

Being in a Mormon wagon train meant adhering to strict rules. The chain of command was well established, and obedience was at a premium. Prayers were to be attended, everyone was to be in bed by nine, "and hogs & dogs to be tied up or shot" at night.

Things were no less organized in Salt Lake Valley. Unlike most towns springing up in the American West, Mormon communities were planned to the hilt: street grids already laid out, rules already in place for who would inhabit which property, how the government would

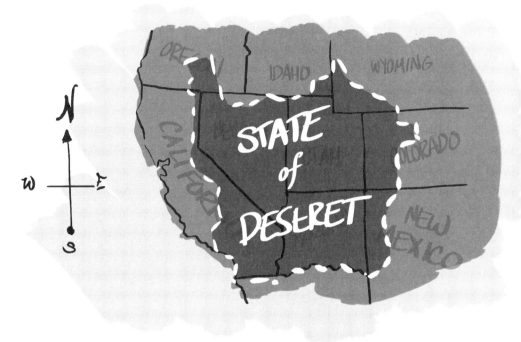

operate, and how natural resources would be used. If you had come to Salt Lake to be your own person, you had come to the wrong place.

But most of those who arrived in Salt Lake Valley were not destined to stay there anyway. Brigham Young had an expansive view of the Mormon kingdom. He proposed the state of Deseret as the Saints' inheritance—an area encompassing all of current-day Utah, most of Nevada and Arizona, Southern California, sizable chunks of Colorado, Wyoming, and New Mexico, and a few slivers of Idaho and Oregon. Often a new batch of Mormon immigrants would just have time to cool their heels before being called to start a new settlement. More than 100 Mormon settlements were founded during the decade following 1847.

COMMUNALISM

One of the main elements that made Mormon settlements so successful was an organized spirit of cooperation. Brigham Young took up Joseph Smith's idea of the United Order and applied it to frontier life, often requiring new settlers to deed their property to the Church and receive an "inheritance" over which they would have "stewardship." Young also established Zion's Cooperative Mercantile Incorporated, which united Mormon merchants so that they could buy and produce goods at a lower cost. Young's goal was to make the Mormons entirely self-sufficient so that they would never be at the mercy of antagonistic neighbors again.

Most instances of the United Order only lasted a few years, but they often provided a boost to new settlements. Probably the most famous and successful of these experiments was called Orderville, established by a clutch of impoverished Mormons who had just failed spectacularly at establishing a settlement in the promisingly named Muddy River, Nevada. The group built a compound with a large-scale dining hall and became almost entirely self-sufficient, producing their own food, clothing, and shelter. None of it was pretty to look at, but it compared very well to the destitution from which they had arisen. Eventually, silver was discovered in the area and what once had been a

WE NEED TO RETHINK COMMUNAL COPYEDITING!

sanctuary from abject poverty started to look backward and poor to its neighbors. Ten years after its founding, the Edmunds-Tucker Act jailed many of Orderville's polygamous leaders and the collective soon fell apart.

Nevertheless, vestiges of communalism still run strong in the LDS Church. One of the main attractions in Salt Lake City today is Welfare Square, the centerpiece of the Church's welfare system. That system cares for people in need while helping them to find ways to support themselves. Every month, Mormons fast from two meals and give the money they would have used on the food to the Church to be used to help the needy. The drive for self-sufficiency also remains a strong part of the Mormon worldview. LDS leaders often counsel Church members to maintain a healthy savings account and to gather food storage in case of emergencies. So make sure you have some Mormon friends before the zombie apocalypse strikes.

SEEKING
STATEHOOD

With the end of the Mexican-American War and the Treaty of Guadalupe Hidalgo in 1848, the United States gained a vast expanse of territory, covering present-day Utah, Arizona, Nevada, and California. As a result, despite their long trek, the Mormons found themselves right back on American soil. Although they had established a government run completely by Church leaders, they decided to see if they could benefit from statehood. When Church leaders arrived in Washington with their petition (a 22-foot-long document), however, Congress was too preoccupied with slavery issues to address the matter.

The Compromise of 1850, a series of legislative measures that reduced the conflict between slave and free states over the status of slavery in lands acquired in the Mexican-American War, granted territorial status to the area named "Utah" (after the native Ute tribe).

The Utah Territory was not as large as the proposed Mormon state of Deseret, but still sizable. President Millard Fillmore appointed a slate of both Mormons and non-Mormons to lead the new territory, with Brigham Young serving as governor.

Tensions sprang up almost immediately. Officials from outside Utah were alarmed by how closely church and state had merged in the territory; Mormons, for their part, felt that the outsiders were destroying the utopia they had built. Conflicts arose between Church members and lay officials and judges, who returned from the territory carrying tales of a "Mormon rebellion." Those accounts, combined with strong anti-polygamy sentiment among Democrats and Republicans (yes, they *did* agree on something once!), finally led to the outbreak of the so-called Utah War.

THE UTAH WAR

Believing the direst of the reports, President James Buchanan appointed Alfred Cumming, a non-Mormon from Georgia, to be Utah's new governor and sent him west with 2,500 soldiers in April 1858 to reassert the federal government's authority. Some members of the Church got wind of the march and hurried back to Salt Lake to warn the leadership.

You might say that the Mormons overreacted to the news. But when you consider that most of them could remember first-hand being driven by mobs and armies from state to state, and when you consider how far they had traveled to practice their religion in peace and what sacrifices they'd made along the way, you can see their point.

Essentially, the Mormons prepared for outright war. Brigham Young declared martial law and sent out marauding parties to slow the advancing troops. The skirmishing lasted only a few months and resulted in few casualties. Young told Church members to hoard their food and supplies, not selling them to outsiders. Then, following Young's instructions, some 35,000 Mormons abandoned their homes in northern Utah, leaving behind a skeleton crew to burn down everything if U.S. troops so much as entered the valley. Church records were hidden; the foundation of the Salt Lake Temple was buried and plowed up so that it would look like a farmer's field. The Saints were going to leave nothing behind for the invaders.

Through some diplomacy on the part of a long-time friend of the Mormons named Thomas L. Kane, a meeting was set up between Church leaders and Cumming, whom Kane persuaded to attend without the army. At the meeting, Brigham Young surrendered control of the territory to Kane and convinced him that the Mormons were good U.S. citizens.

MOUNTAIN MEADOWS MASSACRE

The hysteria that overtook the Mormons during the Utah War had tragic consequences. A migrant group from Arkansas, called the Baker–Fancher Party, was traveling through Utah at the time, on its way to California. Rumors that the party had poisoned a spring of water and that the train was harboring people who had killed a Mormon apostle in Arkansas cast deep suspicion on the travelers.

When the party passed Cedar City in southern Utah, a group of Mormon leaders—under the influence of Brigham's declaration of martial law and teachings from high Church leaders that the wicked needed to be cleansed from the earth to prepare for the Second Coming of Jesus—decided that the wagon train should be destroyed. They set up an attack in conjunction with local Paiute Indians and then disguised local members of the Utah Territory's Nauvoo Legion militia as Native Americans.

The attackers descended upon the wagon train at a place called Mountain Meadows on September 7, 1857, but the travelers managed to hold them off in a five-day siege. Mormon leaders, worried that some in the party had recognized white faces among their attackers and had realized who they were, put together a plan.

On September 11, Mormon militiamen led by Church official John D. Lee approached the embattled Baker–Fancher Party with a white flag and said that they had cut a deal with the Paiutes. If the party would give them their livestock, Lee told the pioneers, the Paiutes would allow them to leave. The migrants agreed and were escorted toward Cedar City by the militia; the men were in one party with a military escort, the women and children in another.

On signal, the militia turned and shot the men, while other militia members attacked the women and children. A total of 120 people were killed that day, all of them buried in shallow graves. Their remains, mauled by wildlife and battered by weather, were found by investigators years later.

POLYGAMY REVISITED

When the Mormons settled in Utah, polygamy became one of their most important theological and cultural identifiers. Declared Apostle George A. Smith, "they are a poor, narrow minded, pinch-backed race of man, who chain themselves to the law of monogamy." (*Deseret News*, April 16, 1856) Church leaders taught unequivocally that one must be part of a polygamous marriage in order to reach the highest level of the Celestial Kingdom. Yet the earthly success of these marriages was mixed. Some older women would advise new plural wives that the best way to have a successful marriage was to give up on romance or tenderness with one's husband, as it would breed only jealousy and disappointment. Often a plural wife's most fulfilling relationships were with her sister wives.

When the Mormons settled in Salt Lake Valley, they thought they had established themselves outside the purview of the United States and its laws. But the U.S. government annexed the area and began working to eradicate Mormon polygamy, which it considered to be—according to the Republican Party platform of 1856—one of the "twin relics of barbarism" (the other being slavery). "It is a scarlet whore," thundered Illinois congressman John McClernand. "It is a reproach to the Christian civilization, and deserves to be blotted out."

But the Mormons were stubborn. They had established plural marriage through great sacrifice; it had become an essential ordinance for salvation, and they weren't about to relinquish it. This was the hill they were willing to die on. And they almost did.

The Civil War distracted the federal government from the issue for a while, giving the Mormons a reprieve. But it wasn't long before a series of laws, culminating in the Edmunds-Tucker Act of 1887, made male polygamists subject to criminal prosecution. Violators could be stripped of the ability to hold public office, serve on a jury, or even vote; any who would not foreswear the practice could be sent to prison. For Mormon men, being incarcerated for plural marriage became a badge of honor (even if it was a crippling burden to the women and children left at home). The government also threatened to confiscate the Church's assets if it continued to condone plural marriage. John Taylor, the third president of the LDS Church (1880–1887) and husband to nine wives, died in hiding.

It was the Church's fourth president, Wilford Woodruff (1889–1898), who in 1890 issued what is often called the Woodruff Manifesto, rescinding Mormon polygamy 38 years after it had been publicly announced. Sort of. The fact was, polygamous marriages continued; they were just much quieter, often conducted outside Utah or U.S. borders—on a steamship, or in Mexico or Canada. Taking advantage of loopholes in the manifesto's language, more than 200 polygamous marriages were solemnized by high Church officials between 1890 and 1903.

When LDS apostle Reed Smoot was elected as a U.S. senator in 1903, an intense spotlight was turned on Mormonism in an attempt to deny him his seat. Smoot himself wasn't a polygamist, but most of his fellow apostles were—and some of them were still performing polygamous marriages. The president of the Church at the time, Joseph F. Smith (1901–1918), had fathered eleven children with his multiple wives since the manifesto. Under the intense outside scrutiny, Smith announced the Second Manifesto: thenceforth, anyone

who married polygamously, or who officiated in such a marriage, would be excommunicated.

The two manifestos shook the Church to its core. Many of its staunchest members had placed all their eggs in the plural marriage basket. Splinter groups soon formed to continue the practice, some of which persist in one form or another to this day. Meanwhile, the LDS Church got on board with the U.S. government and proactively assisted in hunting down and prosecuting polygamists.

Currently, the LDS Church will excommunicate anyone who enters into a polygamous marriage. Nevertheless, the revelation on plural marriage is still a part of the Doctrine and Covenants, and vestiges of the practice still remain in place: a man can be "sealed" to more than one woman in the temple (as in the case of remarriage after a wife's death), but a woman cannot be sealed to more than one man. And many mainstream Mormons believe that they will have to enter a polygamous relationship in the next life in order to attain the top level of salvation, a belief that has never been officially repudiated.

ASSIMILATION

After polygamy was finally dropped, Mormon history consists mainly of how the LDS Church found its way into the mainstream of American culture and how it organized itself into the gigantic, complex, prosperous institution it is today.

For the first half-century of its existence, the Mormon Church was deeply in debt, but through a long and focused process of organization, financial investment, and legal work, it has become wealthy and powerful. Just south of Temple Square in Salt Lake City, Utah, stands a $2-billion megamall with a retractable roof, a river, and high-end shops that the Church had a major hand in developing. It owns an estimated 1 million acres of land in the United States (and plenty more worldwide), as well as insurance companies, real estate companies, publishing companies, radio stations, digital content developers, and universities—the largest and best known of which is Brigham Young University in Provo, Utah; it has also been a major stock holder in such franchise giants as Burger King and Domino's Pizza.

From some perspectives, such deep investment in "the world" would seem to be anathema to a church, but Latter-day Saints often think of prosperity as the

inevitable result of righteousness. It's also worth remembering that the early history of Mormonism is rife with trauma—the kind the Church never wants to go through again. And the best way to avoid that is to have power.

Latter-day Saints like to speak of themselves as a peculiar people, and certainly there are many things that set them apart from the rest of the U.S. population. But the fact is that, in many ways, Mormons have become model Americans. The Church took its first step toward gaining mainstream respectability in 1893, when it sent the Mormon Tabernacle Choir to perform at the World's Fair in Chicago; it took second place. In 1948, President Dwight D. Eisenhower appointed Mormon apostle Ezra Taft Benson as U.S. secretary of agriculture, and he held the post for eight years. In the tumultuous 1960s, Mormons at large refused to participate in the countercultural movement, establishing a clean-cut, straight-arrow, law-abiding image. In contrast to its early politically radical roots, Mormonism took a decidedly conservative stance.

Which brings us to the present … where Mormons are over-represented in the CIA and the FBI; where Mormons hold high political office as a matter of course; where some of the wealthiest people in the United States are Latter-day Saints; and, where, if Mormons move in next door, you can expect property values to go up. That's the journey Mormonism has made: from radical, persecuted church to all-American religion.

The LDS Church has also expanded to become a worldwide movement. During its early years, missionaries found great success in Great Britain and then in Scandinavia. Since then, Central and South America have become homes to major Mormon populations. In fact, the majority of Church membership is now located outside North America. How the Church will evolve to accommodate membership in such diverse areas, cultures, and circumstances is likely to be the biggest challenge it will face in the coming decades.

part 2

LDS SCRIPTURE

THE BOOK OF
MORMON

In a nutshell, the Book of Mormon is a 500+ page text that narrates the religious and political history of two pre-Columbian civilizations in the Western Hemisphere. Or, as the introduction puts it, "It is a record of God's dealings with ancient inhabitants of the Americas and contains the fulness of the everlasting gospel."

The book starts with the story of two Hebrew families leaving Jerusalem around 600 B.C.E., eventually making their way across an ocean to the Americas. Once there, they split into two nations—the Nephites and the Lamanites—that fight with each other for the next eight centuries until the Nephites are finally wiped out. The remaining Lamanites are cited by the Book of Mormon's introduction as being "among the ancestors of the American Indians." Toward the end of the work, a similar story is told about a group of families, called the Jaredites, that leave the scene of the Tower of Babel, travel to the Americas, divide into warring factions, and destroy one another.

But the Book of Mormon is more than just a violent history (and it is *very* violent). According to Moroni, the final contributor, the book was compiled prophetically for the benefit of the people who would live in the Americas during the Last Days: to warn them of the specific difficulties they will face, the particular sins that will tempt them, and the blessings that can be theirs. In other words, even though it was compiled almost 1,500 years ago, the Book of Mormon is aimed directly at current-day inhabitants of North and South America.

In the Latter-day Saint mind, the idea that the Book of Mormon speaks directly to our day, age, and geography bumps it up past the Bible in spiritual import. Yes, you read that right. Though the Bible is definitely considered scripture, in the Latter-day Saint worldview the Book of Mormon is more important. Joseph Smith unabashedly proclaimed,

> **"I told the brethren that the Book of Mormon was the most correct of any book on earth, and the keystone of our religion, and a man would get nearer to God by abiding by its precepts, than by any other book."** (*Introduction: The Book of Mormon*)

Mormons are also more likely to trust the Book of Mormon over the Bible because of their respective pedigrees. It's well known that the writings that make up the Bible have a long and checkered history. Manuscripts were lost and found, translated and mistranslated—and scholars don't always agree on the translations, anyway. And then there was the sausage-making process of compiling the Bible.

The Book of Mormon, on the other hand, was compiled by a prophet (Mormon, for whom the book is named) and funneled through a single God-directed translator: Joseph Smith. Because the words of the Book of Mormon are said to have come though Joseph's seer stone, most Mormons believe—much like Bible literalists—that each word in the Book of Mormon has God's divine stamp of approval. (Its translation into other languages, however, is done by humans.) As Mormonism's eighth Article of Faith states: "We believe the Bible to be the word of God as far as it is translated correctly . . ."

It may seem strange that the Mormon Church would give so much weight to the Book of Mormon when it claims to be a Christian religion. After all, aren't the words of Jesus Christ found only in the Bible? Well, no, Mormons don't think so. About three-quarters of the way

through the Book of Mormon, the resurrected Jesus visits the people in America and gives them many of the teachings that are recorded in the New Testament. He calls apostles and sets up a church that lasts about 200 years. There are also sermons in the Book of Mormon that prophesy Christ's birth and preach parts of his gospel. In other words, the Book of Mormon has a *lot* of Jesus. Indeed, in 1982 the Church gave it a subtitle: "Another Testament of Jesus Christ."

What the Book of Mormon "Did"

The Book of Mormon has been at the center of a lot of controversy. The main conflict is over whether the book is an actual record of a pre-

Columbian American civilization (as most Mormons believe) or a 19th-century text created through one means or another by Joseph Smith. (This controversy is summarized in Part 4: Hot-button Issues.) Plenty of books purporting to be religious scripture have popped up throughout history, but it takes something unique for one to actually take hold—and the Book of Mormon has proven itself successful as scripture, no matter its origins. Although it had literary precursors that presented a similar story and riffed on similar themes, the Book of Mormon fired the American religious imagination in two ways: it sacralized America, and it cracked open the scriptural canon.

The European colonization of America was propelled at least partly by a religious vision; the continent was often framed as a "promised land" for those who wanted to practice their religion freely. Since European settlers were mainly unaware of Native American spiritual traditions, America seemed to them a mythless land, a *tabula rasa* waiting for the imprimatur of Christianity.

But the Book of Mormon changed that. Those who read it saw almost 1,000 years of pre-Columbian, even pre-Christian, American history unfolding before them. And it wasn't a foreign history with strange people and customs; it had deep roots in the Judeo-Christian tradition. The Book of Mormon teaches that Native Americans are at least partially descended from Hebrews in Jerusalem, and are therefore part of the Abrahamic covenant. These Hebrew transplants to America, it is said, had access to early Biblical scripture and developed a uniquely clear understanding of Christ's mission hundreds of years before he came to earth. And, as has already been pointed out, Christ visited these people after his resurrection, and his church was extant on the American continent for hundreds of years before finally falling into apostasy. Thus, the Book of Mormon imbued both America and its indigenous peoples with familiarity to its readers—a place that could be called home, a people that could be called family.

Along with the integration of Judeo-Christian history with that of ancient America came an emboldening promise. As the first Hebrew family settles in America, they are told, "this land is consecrated unto him whom [God] shall bring. And if it so be that they shall serve him according to the commandments which he hath given, it shall be a land of liberty unto them . . ." (2 Nephi 1:7)

The Book of Mormon refers to this promise over and over again, often structuring the narrative around its fulfillment. For example, when the Nephites separate from the Lamanites, Nephi, the leader of the Nephites, writes,

> **And we did observe to keep the judgments, and the statutes, and the commandments of the Lord in all things, according to the law of Moses. And the Lord was with us; and we did prosper exceedingly; for we did sow seed, and we did reap again in abundance."** (2 NEPHI 5:10–11)

Inevitably, however, those who prosper harden their hearts toward God, which causes God to unleash wars, famines, or (heaven help us) heavy taxes upon them until they repent. This process is known in Mormon circles as the "pride cycle."

The prosperity doctrine, explicitly connecting personal righteousness with economic success, has had an energizing effect on Mormons from the beginning. It is one of the reasons why most early Latter-day Saints were so willing to sacrifice so much for Mormonism: they believed that it would all come back to them, that they were helping

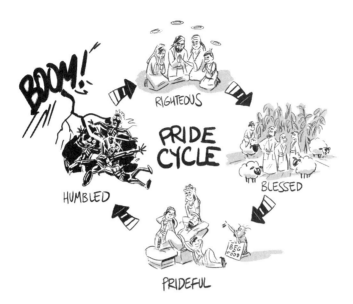

to a build a kingdom that could not be stopped as long as they were obeying the commandments.

In many ways, it seems that their faith was well placed. The Church today has many millions of members and has developed a sizable financial empire. Now Mormons just have to be careful of that *other* part of the pride cycle.

And they really *should*, too, because the destructiveness of pride is a major theme in the Book of Mormon. Moroni is directly addressing those living in the latter days (including Mormons) when he writes,

> For behold, ye do love money, and your substance, and your fine apparel, and the adorning of your churches, more than ye love the poor and the needy, the sick and the afflicted. O ye pollutions, ye hypocrites, ye teachers, who sell yourselves for that which will canker, why have ye polluted the holy church of God? (MORMON 8:37–38)

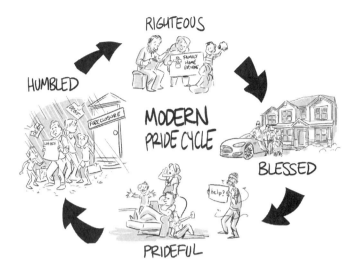

By sacralizing America, the Book of Mormon helped the Latter-day Saints feel at home in this new land and act upon it with confidence, certain that God would prosper them in their righteousness.

But the Book of Mormon did one more audacious thing: it ripped open the scriptural canon. Christianity had been running on the Bible for a long time, and, from the Mormon point of view, had gotten into kind of a rut. By introducing a new book of scripture comparable with the Bible, Joseph Smith posited that God was still interacting with humanity, still revealing new knowledge. As Article of Faith 9 says, "We believe all that God has revealed, all that He does now reveal, and we believe that He will yet reveal many great and important things pertaining to the Kingdom of God."

Lamanites in the Book of Mormon

Mormons have long believed that the indigenous people of Polynesia and North, Central, and South America are Lamanites, principally descended from Lehi (who leads his family out of Jerusalem to the Americas at the beginning of the Book of Mormon). In other words, people "indigenous" to the Americas and Polynesia are believed to be a long lost branch of Israel.

Joseph Smith prophesied that the Lamanites/Native Americans would someday "blossom as the rose" and so sent some of his earliest missionaries to Native American tribes. LDS leaders and missionaries would often tell potential converts in Central America, South America, and Polynesia that they were descendants of Lehi and could find their spiritual history in the Book of Mormon. When the Church started growing by leaps and bounds in those areas, Mormon leaders often referred to Smith's prophecy and to those in the Book of Mormon, saying that they were finally being fulfilled.

But some baggage came along with this story, too.

In the Book of Mormon, skin color is often connected with faithfulness. As the Nephites separate from the Lamanites early in the Book of Mormon, Nephi writes that God

had caused the cursing to come upon them, yea, even a sore cursing, because of their iniquity. . . . [A]s they were white, and exceedingly fair and delightsome, that they might not be enticing unto my people the Lord God did cause a skin of blackness to come upon them. And thus saith the Lord

> **God: I will cause that they shall be loathsome unto thy people, save they shall repent of their iniquities. And cursed shall be the seed of him that mixeth with their seed; for they shall be cursed even with the same cursing.** (2 NEPHI 5:21–23)

In contrast to a miraculous conception of this "curse" (i.e., that they received a darker epidermis by divine means), some Mormon scholars have argued that the change of skin coloration was the genetic result of Lamanite intermarriage with other, darker-skinned indigenous people already living on the American continent. Others have argued that it wasn't the actual skins of the Lamanites that changed color, but the ritual coloring of the animal pelts they wore. However, for a great deal of Mormon history, skin coloration was associated with faithfulness, resulting in some cringe-worthy sermons and publications.

The entire discourse underwent significant revision when DNA studies conducted on Native Americans showed almost no trace of Middle Eastern ancestry (it was mostly Asian). The Church has since backed off its position that the members of Lehi's family are the "principal ancestors of the American Indians," now saying that the family is only "among" their ancestry.

The Book of Mormon's "Story"

Though it has its share of sermons and exhortations, the Book of Mormon is mostly a story: a long, complicated, subplot-ridden nar-

rative that takes more than one read to plumb. Either that, or, as Mark Twain put it, the Book of Mormon is "chloroform in print"—a sleeping aid you can get for free by calling this toll-free number ...

It starts simply enough with the migrating Hebrew family we've already talked about. But when they start reproducing, moving away from home, getting lost, building their own cities, and getting into fights with each other, it's all the reader can do to keep up.

To give you a bit of a head start, here are a few of the Book of Mormon's most prominent characters.

NEPHI.

Probably the book's most popular character, Nephi starts the Book of Mormon with his first-person account of what it was like to head off with the rest of his family into the wilderness after his dad, Lehi, prophesied the destruction of Jerusalem. Nephi is the most spiritual of the siblings and has a bent for leadership, which really gets on his older brothers' nerves. They actually try to kill him a few times, but between the intervention of an angel and a "shock" superpower God briefly gives to Nephi, he manages to survive. He keeps the family together during many years in the wilderness, builds a ship that carries them across the ocean to the Americas, and eventually leads a group of followers away from his brothers' families to start a new nation. This is where the division between the Nephites and the Lamanites begins.

ZENIFF.

Starting out as a virulent Lamanite-hater, Zeniff is sent to scope out a Lamanite settlement in preparation for his army's attack. While there, he discovers that Lamanites are (gasp!) normal people. He tries to stop the attack, accidentally causing the Nephite soldiers to slaughter each other instead. Later he gathers a group of adventurous Nephites to see if they can peacefully inhabit the land Nephi abandoned to the Lamanites so many generations before. The Lamanite king lets him do so, but then allows his own people to plunder Zeniff's settlements, which really confuses poor Zeniff.

ALMA THE ELDER.

Likely growing up in the land Zeniff settled, Alma is a priest for the wicked King Noah (Zeniff's son). But one day a prophet named Abinadi is brought into the throne room for interrogation. Alma's heart is touched by Abinadi's teachings and he tries to save the prophet; instead, King Noah threatens Alma's life, forcing him to hide in the wilderness. While there, Alma writes down Abinadi's teachings and gathers a group of followers who escape from the city just before a Lamanite attack. But the Lamanites later find Alma's group and enslave them for more than a decade before they are able to escape. Alma eventually becomes head of the church in Zarahemla, a major Nephite city.

Alma the Younger.

Alma the Elder's son is rebellious and tries to tear down the church, until an angel appears to him and sets him on the right track. After that, he and the sons of King Mosiah embark on missions to the Lamanites. Alma the Younger goes on to become one of the most written-about prophets in the Book of Mormon, leading battle campaigns, going on missions, getting thrown in jail and then miraculously released, seeing his converts hurled into a pit of fire, going head-to-head with a bunch of apostates (often sealing his victory with a miracle), and dealing with his own rebellious son.

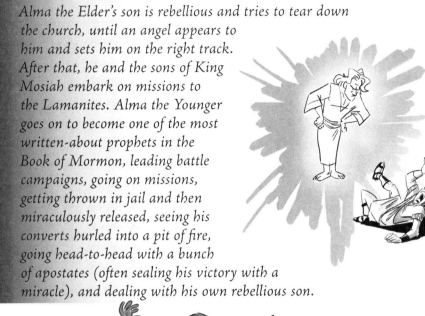

Ammon.

One of the sons of King Mosiah, Ammon is known for winning the admiration of a Lamanite king by chopping the arms off a band of men trying to steal the king's flocks. He converts the king who brings his whole kingdom, and then his father's kingdom, into the church. Having been a violent and murderous people, these new converts bury their weapons as a part of their conversion and suffer several slaughters before Ammon can find a safe place for them in Nephite lands.

CAPTAIN MORONI

...AND THE LATEST IN THE CAPTAIN MORONI SERIES OF ARMORWEAR!

is the Chuck Norris of the Book of Mormon. He becomes the commander of the Nephite armies as the beginning of a long war is descending. But Captain Moroni has a lot of tricks up his sleeve, like outfitting the Nephite soldiers with body armor (the Lamanites prefer to fight commando style); installing the Nephite version of home security (i.e., spiked trenches) around the city walls; and luring the Lamanites out of captured cities with a tantalizingly small army (another one waiting nearby to sneak in the gates). At one point, Captain Moroni writes to the chief judge asking for reinforcements and finds out that the capital has been taken by "king-men." Despite the fact that he's already in a heated battle, he takes a few of his best soldiers, heads back to the capital, starts a popular uprising, and takes the king-men down.

However, Captain Moroni is best remembered for his "title of liberty"—Mormonism's first meme. As a group attempts to install a king in place of the judges, Moroni tears his cloak, writes on it "In memory of our God, our religion, and freedom, and our peace, our wives, and our children," and marches

ADD A CAT!

through the streets to gain support for the judges. You can find a portrait of him hoisting the title of liberty in many LDS chapels.

JESUS CHRIST

*makes a few appearances in the
Book of Mormon: once when
he reveals himself in spirit
form to the Brother of Jared,
and once when he visits
the Nephites just after his
resurrection. However, Jesus
is not a character in the Book of Mormon the same way
he is a character in the New Testament. Instead of being
born, growing up, and developing a ministry as he does
in the New Testament, he descends from the sky in great
glory, with God testifying that Jesus is his son. Jesus's
interactions with the Nephites account for 17 chapters in
the Book of Mormon. He preaches the Sermon on the
Mount, he heals people, he sets up his church, and he
institutes the sacrament. He also delivers the news that
he will soon be visiting "other sheep, which are not of this
land, neither of the land of Jerusalem, neither in any
parts of that land round about whither I have been to
minister" (3 Nephi 16:1) — opening the possibility that yet
more scripture may come to light of Jesus's visits to other
parts of the world.*

THE THREE NEPHITES.

*While Jesus is setting up his church among the Nephites,
he chooses 12 apostles. He asks them the wish of their
heart, and three say they want to remain on earth to
teach the gospel, which Jesus grants. The Three Nephites
have since become the stuff
of Mormon urban legend,
showing up as hitchhikers
who, before disappearing
from the back seat, admonish
drivers to gather food storage,
or plowing a field for a sick
and grieving Mormon farmer, or
protecting Mormon missionaries.*

THE BROTHER OF JARED.

His story starts at the biblical Tower of Babel. When the languages are confounded, he prays that he and his family and friends can keep theirs, which God grants. They form a group called the Jaredites and head off to the American continent in football-shaped ships lit with stones touched by God's finger. The Brother of Jared has the dubious distinction of being chewed out by God for three straight hours for neglecting to pray for four years.

MORMON,

for whom the book is named, is a prophet warrior who dumps his job as commander of the Nephite armies when he realizes that they aren't going to repent and takes up the job of editor and redactor of the Book of Mormon. Essentially, he's the guy sitting in the room with all the Nephite records stacked around him, choosing what will get into the Book of Mormon and what won't, adding his commentary here and there, and even writing a small book of his own. He engraves this collection onto a set of golden plates.

MORONI

is Mormon's son and becomes caretaker of the plates when his father dies in the last battle that destroys the Nephite nation. As Moroni runs from Lamanite armies, he adds a few thoughts of his own at the end of the plates and eventually buries them in the Hill Cumorah. More than 1,000 years later, he will appear to Joseph Smith and guide him to those plates.

WOMEN.

Have you noticed something? Like how there haven't been any women on this list? That's because the Book of Mormon is singularly female-free. Only six are mentioned by name, and three of them are from the Bible (Eve, Mary, and Sarah—Abraham's wife). The other three are Sariah, Abish, and Isabel. Sariah is the mother of Nephi. Abish is a Lamanite servant who saves Ammon's life. Isabel is a harlot with whom one of Alma the Younger's sons passes some time. Women show up collectively in other places, such as when a group of young soldiers say that they were saved from death because they had faith in the gospel precepts their mothers had taught them; or when Ammon's women and children converts are being thrown into a pit of fire; or when comely Nephite women are sent to beg for a Lamanite army's mercy; or when women and children are being forced to eat the flesh of their husbands and fathers; or when some young women are stolen away by King Noah's priests. Few books fail the Bechdel test* more utterly than the Book of Mormon.

*The Bechdel test, named for cartoonist Alison Bechdel, judges a movie or book based on whether or not it contains a scene in which two or more female characters talk to each other about anything besides a man.

FAIL.

One of the most interesting things about the Book of Mormon is the fact that it has a sad ending. The Nephite nation is wiped completely off the face of the planet during the last chapters, and it is destroyed precisely because of the Nephites' unwillingness to repent. Mormon, who leads an army during the final clash, describes it as follows:

And it came to pass that my people, with their wives and their children, did now behold the armies of the Lamanites marching towards them; and with that awful fear of death which fills the breasts of all the wicked, did they await to receive them. (MORMON 6:7)

Then, by the next day, their flesh, and bones, and blood lay upon the face of the earth, being left by the hands of those who slew them to molder upon the land . . . . (MORMON 6:15)

The entire purpose of the Book of Mormon, according to Mormon, is to testify that Jesus Christ is the Son of God, and to warn the people of today that they could share the Nephites' fate if they don't repent. And so—though a bit of a downer—the ending is entirely appropriate.

But the book doesn't quite end there. Moroni, Mormon's son, adds a few sentences that have become the most quoted words in Mormonism. If you ever sit down to talk with a pair of Mormon missionaries, there is a 100 percent chance that you will hear this verse:

> And when ye shall receive these things [i.e. the Book of Mormon], I would exhort you that ye would ask God, the Eternal Father, in the name of Christ, if these things are not true; and if ye shall ask with a sincere heart, with real intent, having faith in Christ, he will manifest the truth of it unto you, by the power of the Holy Ghost. (MORONI 10:4)

This is how one develops a "testimony" of the truth of the Book of Mormon: through prayer and personal revelation. There is some debate in LDS circles about whether this "truth" refers only to the Book of Mormon's truth as scripture (much as the Book of Job can be scripture while still being fiction) or if it also refers to the book's historical truth. Though Church leaders have almost always insisted that the Book of Mormon is historical, its ultimate value to Mormons lies in its spiritual teachings.

THE DOCTRINE AND COVENANTS

O rganizing a church is no small task, which is why you want only the best people on your team. For Joseph Smith, that meant Jesus. The Doctrine and Covenants is a series of revelations that Smith is said to have received on various topics—from how to conduct a baptism (immersion only), to what can be used for the sacrament (anything, though the Church prescribes bread and water), to where Zion should be built (Independence, Missouri), to whose seer stone is the best (Joseph's).

Originally organized by topic, the Doctrine and Covenants is now organized mostly chronologically, begin-ning with Joseph's earliest encoun-ter with the angel who led him to the golden plates, and ending with a 1978 announcement (added to the Doctrine and Covenants in 1981) that allows all worthy LDS males to hold the priesthood no matter their skin color or race.

The Doctrine and Covenants is where most of Mormonism's unique beliefs and practices have root. In it you can find descriptions of the United Order, as well as the tithing system (giving one-tenth of your income to the Church); marriage practices (including the polygamous kind); beliefs about the afterlife (hell is called "outer darkness," and its entrance requirements are very strict, while heaven is made up of three degrees); and the Word of Wisdom (no coffee, tea, tobacco, alcohol, or excessive meat).

Joseph Smith received these revelations in a variety of ways. Sometimes he used the Urim and Thummim, sometimes his seer stone, and sometimes he would simply dictate the revelation while a scribe wrote it down. But one thing that ties these revelations together is that most of them were answers to questions—a necessary prerequisite to revelation.

Questions must precede revelation because Mormons, like existentialists, believe that every human soul is "free to choose," as Mormon pop music composer Michael McLean put it (or "condemned to choose," as French philosopher Jean-Paul Sartre less optimistically put it). The agency of a human soul is so complete, so total, that one-third of God's children chose Satan over Jehovah *while in the presence of God*. We are irrevocably our own shapers.

Mormons believe that God is bound by pre-existing principles that order the cosmos. And since human agency is one of those principles, there is often little God can do directly about human behavior, from the honorable to the horrific. God can only work through people's agency.

This principle has been the propelling force behind Mormon history. Heavenly beings appeared to Joseph Smith *because* he was actively asking questions. Most of the revelations recorded in the Doctrine and Covenants came about *because* of questions either Joseph or the people around him were asking.

For instance, it is an oft-told story that Joseph Smith's first wife, Emma, was getting tired of cleaning up the floor after church meetings,

as it was always covered in tobacco spit. She asked Joseph to ask Jesus about it, and that's how the Word of Wisdom (Section 89) came about. An even more extreme example is Section 113, which starts as follows:

> **Who is the Stem of Jesse spoken of in the 1st, 2d, 3d, 4th, and 5th verses of the 11th chapter of Isaiah?**
> **Verily thus saith the Lord: It is Christ.**
>
> *(D&C 113:1–2)*

It may seem odd that Jesus was brought in on such details, but that was the way Joseph Smith worked. He had a direct line, and he was willing to use it. In fact, the earlier sections of the Doctrine and Covenants are for the most part very personal. Individual members would approach Smith to know God's will concerning them and he would receive a revelation, which would be written down and handed to them. Soon Joseph realized the value of the revelations and had them recorded in revelation books the Church still has today.

It is the resurrected, deified Jesus who speaks through Joseph Smith in most of the Doctrine and Covenants. But instead of the scrappy, homeless mystic of the New Testament, Jesus is in the role of organizer and divine managerial consultant.

Of the 138 sections of the Doctrine and Covenants, 135 come through Joseph Smith, one comes through Brigham Young, and one comes through Joseph F. Smith (Joseph Smith's nephew, the Church's sixth president). The other section is a eulogy for Joseph and Hyrum Smith (his brother). As the Church has grown, direct, scriptural revelation that applies to the entire church has decreased dramatically. The most recent addition to the Doctrine and Covenants came in 1981, when the 1978 announcement extending priesthood to all worthy male Church members was added as an "official declaration."

Community of Christ (formerly the Reorganized Church of Jesus Christ of Latter Day Saints) has been much more willing to add sections to its version of the Doctrine and Covenants, with a total of 166. Other Mormon-rooted denominations, such as the Strangites, the Temple Lot group, and the Cutlerites, stick with earlier versions of the Doctrine and Covenants.

THE PEARL OF GREAT PRICE

The shortest book in the Mormon scriptural canon (clocking in at 61 pages), the Pearl of Great Price is like the DVD extras for the Bible. Did you know that Abraham was almost sacrificed by a heathen priest? Or that Adam and Eve's fall was a *good* thing? Or that Enoch led a city so righteous that it was caught up into heaven?

The Pearl of Great Price is basically a collection of writings from Joseph Smith that didn't seem to fit anywhere else. It includes pieces of his translation of the Bible, his translation of some Egyptian papyri, a bit of his own history, and the LDS Church's articles of faith.

The Book of Moses

The first book in the Pearl of Great Price, the Book of Moses, originated from Joseph Smith's "inspired translation" of the Bible. Smith went through the Bible verse by verse, tweaking a few words here and there, and sometimes adding whole chapters. None of this was done by scholarly means, but rather by revelatory means. After his

SHE ATE IT!
LET'S ROLL!!!

death, Emma Smith gave a manuscript of his translation to the Reorganized Church of Jesus Christ of Latter Day Saints, which published it in 1867 The LDS Church has never gotten around to integrating it except through the excerpts in the Pearl of Great Price and through footnotes in the Bible.

The Book of Moses is like the director's cut of the first five chapters of Genesis. It contextualizes the creation story as an extended vision given to Moses and adds a few details. For example, God reveals that all things were created spiritually before they were created physically, that there are many more worlds than just earth, and that Cain killed Abel as a result of a little chat Cain had with Satan.

Probably the most game-changing concept in the Book of Moses is a single line from Eve, who, while reflecting on eating the forbidden fruit, says, "Were it not for our transgression we never should have had seed, and never should have known good and evil, and the joy of our redemption, and the eternal life which God giveth unto all the obedient." (Moses 5:11) In other words, the fall of Adam and Eve was actually an essential part of humankind's progression, rather than the tragedy Christianity often casts it as.

The Book of Moses also dedicates a few chapters to the story of Enoch, in which he has his own vision that reveals God's emotional connection with humankind.

Joseph Smith—Matthew

This brief book is Joseph Smith's translation of Matthew 23:39 and Matthew 24, to which he adds about 450 words.

The Book of Abraham

In July 1835, a touring exhibit of four mummies and accompanying papyri stopped in Kirtland, Ohio, then headquarters of the Mormon Church. After examining them, Smith bought the mummies and their papyri and then revealed that the papyri contained "the writings of Abraham, while he was in Egypt" as well as some writings from Joseph of Egypt. He set to work translating them and had a document ready by 1835, though it wasn't published until 1842.

A first-person narrative by Abraham, the Book of Abraham starts with an angel of God saving him from being sacrificed by a priest (because Abraham had the unpopular view of objecting to child sacrifice). Then he heads out of town and ends up in Ur.

While there, Abraham receives a revelation that has affected Mormon theology to its core. He sees what Mormons now call the "pre-mortal life" where spirits live with God. "We will make an earth whereon these may dwell," God says. "And we will prove them herewith, to see if they will do all things whatsoever the Lord their God shall command them." (Abraham 3:24–25) Then the gods (yes, *gods*) are described building the earth much as it is described in Genesis, except that instead of dividing each labor into "days," they are divided into "times," which gives Mormons flexibility when talking about the age of the earth.

The Book of Abraham is unique among LDS standard works in that it includes Egyptian-type images—or "facsimiles," as they are called. One is of the priest's attempted sacrifice of Abraham. Another is a hypocephalus, a disk-shaped inscription traditionally placed beneath the heads of ancient Egyptian corpses to guide their spirits in the afterlife. The third is of Abraham sitting on Pharaoh's throne expounding on astronomy. Appended to each of these images are explanations of the elements, such as: "Designed to represent the pillars of heaven, as understood by the Egyptians" and "Contains writings that cannot be revealed unto the world; but is to be had in the Holy Temple of God."

After Joseph Smith translated the Book of Mormon, he said that an angel took back the golden plates. Thus, no one else could ever complete a scholarly translation of the plates to compare with his. But the Book of Abraham is a different story.

When Smith died, the mummies and the papyri were dispersed and eventually thought to be lost. In 1966, however, a professor from the University of Utah discovered some of the papyri in the archives of the New York Metropolitan Museum of Art (identifying them by the distinctive "sacrifice" facsimile). This discovery led to more discoveries, and soon the papyri were made available to the public, which gave scholars a chance to analyze them.

What they found was that the papyri had nothing to do with Abraham. They actually contained funerary texts paralleling the Egyptian Book of the Dead and Book of Breathings. Thus, while Joseph Smith interpreted the main elements of the "sacrifice" image as representing the priest, Abraham, and the angel of the Lord, Egyptologists interpreted them as representing "The god Anubis . . . effecting the resurrection of Osiris," "Osiris coming to life on his couch," and "The soul of Osiris" respectively.

THE ANGEL OF THE LORD OR THE SOUL OF OSIRIS?

IDOLATRUOUS PRIEST OF ELKENAH OR THE GOD ANUBIS?

ABRAHAM BEING SACRIFICED OR OSIRIS COMING TO LIFE?

These discoveries and competing translations threw a monkey wrench into the discourse around the Book of Abraham. Critics said it was proof that Joseph Smith made up the Book of Abraham (and probably the Book of Mormon, too). Church scholars rushed to point out that these were not *all* the papyri to which Smith had access—perhaps the Abraham papyrus is still lost. They also argued that Joseph might have used the papyri simply as a catalyst for receiving Abraham's words through revelation—much as he had apparently used the golden plates to receive the Book of Mormon.

The controversy around the Book of Abraham continues to be the subject of much debate in Mormon circles.

Joseph Smith—History

This book contains excerpts from writings Joseph Smith published in the Mormon newspaper *Times and Seasons* about his early spiritual experiences. LDS missionaries often quote from it when teaching potential converts about the founder of the faith. Much of its content is covered at the beginning of Part 1 in this book.

Articles of Faith

Extracted from a letter Joseph Smith wrote in 1842 to a newspaper editor who had asked for information about the Church, this list serves as a starting point for people who want to know what Mormons believe. While it leaves out some significant doctrines—such as the eternal nature of marriage, the pre-mortal life, and the human potential to become gods—the Articles do include some very distinctive doctrines—such as the idea that people are punished for their own sins "and not for Adam's transgression," that there will be a literal gathering of Israel, and that the "New Jerusalem" will be built on the American continent.

" WE BELIEVE IN BEING HONEST, TRUE...

...CHASED BY AN ELEPHANT! " *

* MORMONS FIND THIS JOKE VERY FUNNY AS IT IS A PLAY ON THE FIRST FEW LINES OF THE 13TH ARTICLE OF FAITH:

WE BELIEVE IN BEING HONEST, TRUE, **CHASTE, BENEVOLENT,** VIRTUOUS, AND IN DOING GOOD TO ALL MEN; INDEED, WE MAY SAY THAT WE FOLLOW THE ADMONITION OF PAUL...

ROTATING SCRIPTURE

REVELATIONS
RECEIVED

(NOT TO
SCALE)

I t was pointed out in the Doctrine and Covenants section that, despite having an "open canon" (a willingness to accept additional scripture), the LDS Church has not added anything to its scriptures since 1981. (The last revelation to be added before that was in 1918). Compared to the early days of the Church, when scriptural revelations were being received on an almost weekly basis, things have slowed to a glacial pace.

However, Mormons consider the inspired words of the current prophet and apostles to be scripture. "And whatsoever they shall speak when moved upon by the Holy Ghost shall be scripture, shall be the will of the Lord, shall be the mind of the Lord, shall be the word of the Lord, shall be the voice of the Lord, and the power of God unto salvation." (D&C 68:4)

This belief creates the environment for a kind of rotating canon, where new scripture is created on a monthly basis—and relegated to the archives just as quickly. This happens in the Church's magazines: the *Ensign* (targeted at North American Mormons) and the *Liahona* (targeted at international Mormons). Latter-day Saints often say that articles published in these magazines contain what the prophets want us to know right *now*. Sometimes a church-wide Sunday lesson will focus on a particular talk published in the *Ensign*.

General conference, a semi-annual gathering of Mormons in Salt Lake City to hear the general authorities of the Church speak, also produces a kind of time-stamped scripture. It often surprises non-Mormons to see how willing Latter-day Saints are to sit through 10 hours of sermons over the course of general conference weekend. But from the Mormon point of view, they are hearing the latest from the heavens in real time. The conference is God speaking directly to the Saints, giving them the tools they need to deal with today's world. The issue of the *Ensign* that contains the latest conference proceedings becomes well thumbed over the next six months as people search out counsel relevant to their lives. Then, when the next conference comes up, the whole process starts over again.

The feeling of always having a connection with God's will is a comforting and empowering one for Mormons. Rather than having to extrapolate their beliefs and

behaviors from ancient texts alone, they can always know exactly what God wants them to do.

But the frequent revision of Church guidance can also leave behind a bit of mess. Reading the sermons of past Mormon leaders will sometimes reveal ideas that, according to contemporary standards, seem backward or even uninspired. Indeed, one can find idiosyncratic opinions on marriage, racial theories, homosexuality, and gender roles just by flipping through old conference reports or *Ensign* issues. And so there is a cultural willingness to ignore certain sermons when they become irrelevant or even a little embarrassing. They may be dismissed as being the speaker's opinion—rooted in the speaker's cultural zeitgeist—rather than inspired counsel. So, yes, the sermon of a Mormon leader can be considered inspired counsel during one decade and "only his opinion" in the next. Overall, it's a process that keeps Church members on the same page when wrestling with contemporary issues.

part 3

MORMON LIFE

A Mormon CAN OFTEN TELL within the first few minutes of an interaction if a stranger is also a Mormon. Once that connection is made, it is as if the two share a secret language that allows them to communicate comfortably and efficiently. What makes Mormons so readily recognizable to each other? How do they build affinity so quickly? There are two basic reasons: 1) being a Mormon is like being in the army; and 2) being a Mormon is like being in a great big family.

Go TO A MORMON SACRAMENT MEETING, and you'll see both of these elements at work. At the front of the chapel sit three men: the bishop and his two counselors. They are in charge, and everyone knows it. If the bishop calls on you to do something—from giving a prayer to teaching Sunday school—you do it (though he is unlikely to tell you to drop and give him 20 pushups). But then look at the congregation. They're greeting each other, asking after each other's families, and calling each other brother and sister. If you happen to come on a "fast Sunday" (the first Sunday of every month when the congregation comes fasting), you'll see various people walk up to the podium and, with no prior rehearsal, tell the congregation about their most recent spiritual experiences, which are often very personal.

Stick AROUND FOR SUNDAY SCHOOL, and you'll see that everyone knows their place and their role. The three members of the Primary presidency (the children's organization) have already slipped out of sacrament meeting to prepare for "sharing time" (when all the children get together to sing and give each other little sermons). The librarian is busy making copies for the Sunday school teachers. Home teachers are making appointments with the families they are in charge of. Teens and adults are scurrying off to their classes. It quickly becomes evident that this "family" has a very definite hierarchy. Indeed, if you ask someone a question that is out of his or her stewardship, he or she will know exactly whom to refer you to—the next person up the chain of command. Perhaps your question is best suited to the compassionate service leader; if not her, perhaps it's appropriate for a counselor in the Relief Society presidency—or maybe the Relief Society president herself. If you need to go higher, you'll be talking to the bishop.

MORMON AT 2 O'CLOCK! INITIATE LDS PROTOCOL!

LDS CHURCH:
ORGANIZATION
AND COMMUNITY

A high degree of organization permeates every aspect of the LDS Church. As Joseph Smith once said to a gathering of high priests: "Organize yourselves; prepare every needful thing; and establish a house, even a house of prayer, a house of fasting, a house of faith, a house of learning, a house of glory, a house of order, a house of God." (D&C 88:119) Members are frequently reminded that "obedience is the first law of heaven."

At the top of the Church's org chart is the president and his two counselors (called the First Presidency). Beneath them is the Quorum of the Twelve Apostles. Beneath them are the seven presidents of the Seventy, who preside over the Quorums of the Seventy. Each member of the Seventy presides over a particular area of the world, having stewardship over a collection of stake presidents (a stake is like

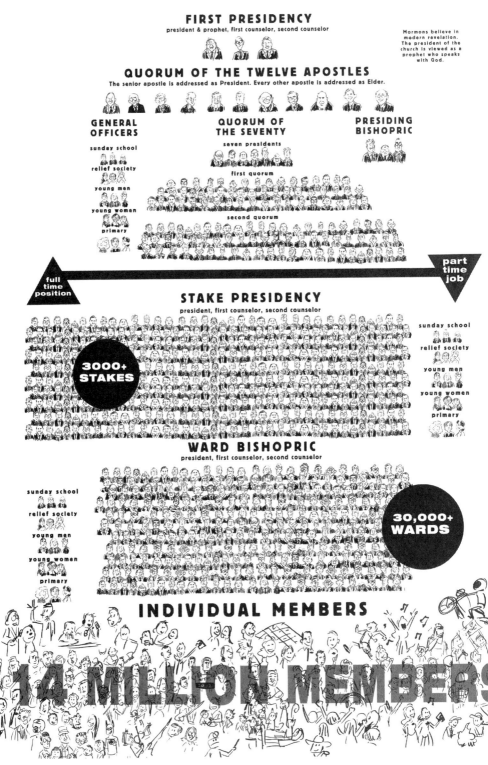

THE MORMON HIERARCHY

FIRST PRESIDENCY
president & prophet, first counselor, second counselor

Mormons believe in modern revelation. The president of the church is viewed as a prophet who speaks with God.

QUORUM OF THE TWELVE APOSTLES
The senior apostle is addressed as President. Every other apostle is addressed as Elder.

GENERAL OFFICERS
sunday school
relief society
young men
young women
primary

QUORUM OF THE SEVENTY
seven presidents

first quorum

second quorum

PRESIDING BISHOPRIC

full time position

part time job

STAKE PRESIDENCY
president, first counselor, second counselor

3000+ STAKES

sunday school
relief society
young men
young women
primary

WARD BISHOPRIC
president, first counselor, second counselor

sunday school
relief society
young men
young women
primary

30,000+ WARDS

INDIVIDUAL MEMBERS

14 MILLION MEMBERS

a diocese) who each preside over a collection of wards (the Mormon term for a congregation) which is presided over by a bishop.

Each and every one of the people in this main line of authority is male. Mormons believe that in order to officially act with God's authority, one must hold the priesthood. Today still, only men are allowed to hold the priesthood. (Yes, there is controversy about this—see Part 4.)

In addition to main authoritative bodies, there are also "auxiliary" organizations, such as the Primary, the Relief Society, the Sunday school, and the youth programs. The officers of the Primary, Relief Society, and Young Women's programs are female. The rest of the positions are populated by males.

A lot of organizational terms are being thrown around here, so here's a quick summary:

- **STAKE:** a collection of wards
  WARD: a Mormon congregation
- **BISHOP:** the head of a ward
- **RELIEF SOCIETY:** the women's organization
- **HIGH PRIESTS QUORUM:** a priesthood organization usually meant for males over 50 and for those who hold high leadership positions
- **ELDERS QUORUM:** a priesthood organization usually meant for males 18–50
- **PRIMARY:** the children's organization
- **YOUNG WOMEN:** the organization for teenage girls, divided into classes called "Beehives," "Mia Maids," and "Laurels"
- **YOUNG MEN:** the organization for teenage boys, divided into priesthood roles called "deacons," "teachers," and "priests"

> + **SUNDAY SCHOOL:** just what it sounds like
> + **HOME TEACHING:** a program in which priesthood holders visit the ward's families in their homes each month
> + **VISITING TEACHING:** a program in which Relief Society members visit the women in their homes each month

Church Meetings

Mormons attend a three-hour block of meetings each Sunday—usually a sacrament meeting first, where the entire congregation meets to take communion and listen to sermons delivered by congregation members. There is also an hour of Sunday school with co-ed classes. Then the sexes split up: women over 18 go to Relief Society, girls 12–17 go to Young Women, and men and teenage boys go to their priesthood quorums. The children go to Primary, which is a mix of classroom instruction, activities, and a large group meeting with singing and brief sermons.

If your only exposure to Mormonism has been through *The Book of Mormon* musical, *South Park* episodes, or Bill Maher comedy routines, you might think that LDS church meetings are filled with curious—even wacky—stuff. It's true that something quirky might pop up now and then from a self-styled doctrinal expert in the ward. But the fact is, most of what's said in a Mormon meeting would pass muster in any Christian congregation. It's usually stuff about families—how to strengthen them, how to protect them, how to make yours better. There's stuff about being a better neighbor and about obeying church authority, God, and the commandments, all of it topped with handwringing about the spiritual decay of today's world, the immorality of the media, and the dangers of Internet pornography.

Mormons cycle through the same curriculum set every four years, covering the Old Testament one year, the New Testament the next, the Book of Mormon after that, and finally the Doctrine and Covenants and Pearl of Great Price. The great majority of these lessons focus on the basics of Mormonism and its behavior codes. So though Mormons, if pressed, will admit to all the weird beliefs that outsiders love to talk about—the Garden of Eden is in Missouri! God lives near a planet called Kolob!—it's likely that they've never actually discussed them in church. Nope. Mormon meetings probably aren't nearly as exciting as you might think.

Community Life

Even if church meetings aren't always exciting, a Mormon ward can still be a great place to live. Its various organizations are highly responsive to the needs of ward members, especially if the home teaching and visiting teaching programs are running well. If you need help moving, just call the elder's quorum president, who will gather a group of men and teens to get your boxes and furniture packed in record time. The Relief Society is particularly adept at providing meals and cleaning house for people who are sick or having a baby. The Young Women and Young Men's organizations can provide help with outdoor work and babysitting. Any member of a ward can have access to these resources, which can make trying times much more bearable.

The Church also has a welfare system that can help a family support itself if a parent becomes unemployed or disabled. In addition to the larger welfare program, Mormons fast from two meals each month and give the money they would have spent on those meals to the bishop, who uses it to help ward families that have fallen on hard times.

The Same Wavelength

This high level of organization also affects the Church's curriculum and media. In the mid-20th century, a major endeavor was undertaken by the Church to "correlate" all of its material, from scriptures to slideshows, from lesson manuals to magazine content. The goal was to make sure that all branches of the Church in all parts of the world were working with essentially the same texts at essentially the same time, and that all those texts supported each other in one grand narrative. Before correlation, Church manuals might have been authored by a particular person, complete with his or her unique writing voice and underlying philosophies. After correlation, all official

Church curriculum was—and is—assembled by teams of writers, researchers, and curriculum specialists. Then it is vetted by committees that include the highest-ranking Church authorities.

So, one of the reasons two Mormons who are otherwise strangers can establish rapport so quickly is that they have been thinking about literally the same gospel principles during the past week, whether they live in Portugal, Pakistan, or Peru. They've been on the same gospel "wavelength": hearing the same lessons, delivering the same home teaching message, listening to the same conference talks, and likely giving similar comments in their church classes.

The structure of every ward is also the same, so one Mormon can say to another, "I'm the second counselor in the elder's quorum," and the other will know exactly what that calling entails and what it likely means about the person's church activity. People who have been in the Church a long time will have held a number of different callings, which often enables them to say, "Ah, yes, I remember having that calling," and immediately start swapping war stories.

This all-permeating organizational focus may seem a bit Borg-ish (after the hive-mind cyborg race in *Star Trek: The Next Generation*)—indeed, some Mormons even refer to the Church as the "Morg"—but these structures also provide an opportunity for Church members to connect with each other in significant ways.

Volunteerism

WE'D LIKE TO CALL YOU AS WARD ORGANIST!

While upper-level Church callings (such as apostle and seventy) come with some kind of remuneration (though a tight lid is kept on how exactly that works), local-level Church callings are unpaid and drawn from the congregation. Thus, your next-door neighbor might be your fishing buddy one week and your bishop the next (and he'll likely remain so for the next five years). When you consider the hours that go into some higher-level local callings, such as bishop and Relief Society president, the fact that these positions are staffed by volunteers is remarkable. Being a Relief Society president or bishop can easily eat up 20 hours a week. Stake callings can take even more time.

This volunteerism means that everyone who works in a local church position is untrained. There is no such thing as a Mormon seminary for training bishops or Relief Society presidents. Everyone who is called brings with them their unique set of abilities, experiences, and weaknesses. Thus, there is always a learning curve, and the best person for a particular calling may be working in another position. This setup leads to a lot of unpolished, even amateurish job performances, with some volunteers getting by on the patience of their ward members. However, it also brings a set of unique, and sometimes memorable, flavors to each ward.

Congregation members will often remember how their ward changed under the leadership of particular bishops: this guy was funny and generous, that guy was solemn but organized. Girls may remember the CEO, the housewife, and the Ph.D. who worked together to run their Young Women's program. Boys may remember how one Young Men's leader was all about campouts and carving, while another had a great cabin and lots of snowmobiles. The fact that all of these people are volunteers makes their work a labor of love. Warm relationships often form between those who serve and those who are served. The ward becomes like a big family.

Change, Alienation, and Testimony

Which is why it can be so jarring, even grief-inducing, when the organizational arm of the Church makes changes. For example, when a ward gets too large, the stake leaders may split it. This may not seem like a big deal, but wards are formed on the parish model: instead of finding a congregation that suits them, Mormons are expected to go to church with the people who live around them. Church is a major

source of members' friendships and socializing. (Indeed, the stress of moving to another state, or even another country, is greatly reduced because Mormons know that they will find a built-in support system wherever they go.) So when a ward is split, it may mean losing some of your best friends. Sure you may still live close to each other, but you don't interact with them every Sunday anymore.

People who stop attending church—what Mormons call "going inactive"—often experience a similar repercussion in their lives: LDS friends begin to drift away, partly because the bass beat of correlated programs and time together in church no longer connects them.

But the alienation can go deeper than that. Another reason two Mormons who are otherwise strangers can come to trust each other quickly is that they share a core belief set: that Joseph Smith was a prophet, that the Book of Mormon is scripture, that Mormonism is God's true church, and that the current prophet speaks for God. According to the oft-repeated line of reasoning, if the Book of Mormon is true (a testimony of which one can gain from prayer), then Joseph Smith, who produced the Book of Mormon, is a prophet of God. If Joseph Smith is a prophet of God, then the church he established must be true. If the Church is true, then the current prophet must be called of God as well, and we should obey his counsel.

The Mormon identity, belief system, and morality code are built on this foundational reasoning. Most Mormons believe and behave as they do because they have a "testimony" that these core principles are true. Going inactive can breach the connection with that testimony, compromise the belief set, and alienate one from the community.

All In or All Out

Indeed a *lot* of behavior grows from a Mormon testimony. Mormons are required to pay ten percent of their income to the Church. They are also supposed to obey the Word of Wisdom: a health code that prohibits coffee, tea, alcohol, tobacco, and illicit drugs. (Many conser-

vative Mormons also insist that caffeine is off limits). Any kind of sex outside of marriage can get you excommunicated. Plus there are the many hours Mormons spend on church work. With all the council meetings, presidency meetings, home teaching and visiting teaching appointments, Primary activities, mid-week Young Men and Young Women activities, temple nights, and service projects, you're lucky to get through a week with only five hours of church work. For Mormons, church isn't a place you go on Sunday, it's *life.*

This is part of an "all in or all out" attitude in Mormon culture. A Catholic who uses birth control and attends only Mass on Easter and Christmas is still a Catholic. A Jew who is an atheist is still a Jew. But if a Mormon doesn't go to church, has a sip of whisky now and then, and doesn't pay tithing, is he or she still a Mormon? A number of Latter-day Saints would say no. The gospel is portrayed not as a buffet where you can pick and choose what you want, but as a sit-down dinner where you must clean your plate.

Faith Crises

So when Mormons experience doubt about the core claims of the Church, their entire world can come apart: not only their view of the Church, but their view of themselves and reality. Sometimes their entire worldview can be brought down with a single stroke. For example, if a Mormon is discomfited enough by Joseph Smith's polygamy, he or she may decide that Smith wasn't a prophet at all. This would mean that the Book of Mormon isn't scripture and that the LDS Church isn't true, which would mean that the entire narrative upon which the questioning Mormon has built his or her life could be false. "Am I really a child of God?" he or she may ask. "Is there actually a plan of salvation?" "Is Jesus real?" "Is there an afterlife?" "Are all these rules I've sacrificed for my entire life just made up?" Suddenly it's all up in the air—the Mormon version of existential despair.

And that's just what's going on *inside* the doubting Mormon. On the outside, everything is likely to be falling apart as well. For example, one of the most stressful things a Mormon couple can undergo is a crisis of faith by one spouse. Because Mormons believe that marriage is essential for exaltation, if one partner questions his or her faith, the other may see their entire future coming down around their ears. What will happen to the family? Will they still be sealed in the heavens, or will the believing spouse have to marry someone else in order to get into the Celestial Kingdom? A wife may interpret her husband's doubt as an attack on their marriage, as a renunciation of his love for her. Children may interpret a parent's doubt as an abandonment of them. Friends and ward members at first may regard the doubter as someone who needs counseling with the bishop; but if the counseling doesn't work, the doubter may been seen as a wolf in sheep's clothing—someone to be avoided lest his or her doubt, like a virus, infects them as well.

Although some Mormons end up leaving the Church (or at least disassociating from it) via this route, others follow a "stages of faith" path. By this process, as theorized by psychologists such as James Fowler, the doubting Church member uses the period of analysis and soul-searching to build, from the ground up, a personal faith and spiritual worldview that ends up resonating with the core principles of Mormonism—often at a deeper level than before.

It's important to note that not all Mormons go through a "faith crisis," though it has become more common with the advent of the Internet. It's also important to note that the Mormon Church has shown an ability to appeal to those who are raised LDS, those who have converted from another religion, and those who have gone through a faith crisis. It has developed the resources and experience to work with people in many different life stages and faith contexts.

MISSIONS

As the *Lectures on Faith* teaches, "a religion that does not require the sacrifice of all things never has the power sufficient to produce the faith necessary unto life and salvation." (6:7) Nowhere is that ideal more evident in Mormon life than it is in missionary work.

Samuel Smith, Joseph Smith's younger brother, became Mormonism's first missionary when, at age 22, he lugged a knapsack full of newly printed copies of the Book of Mormon for 40 miles to sell at any house he encountered. He eventually sold one to Phineas Young, who gave it to his brother Brigham Young, who eventually became the second president of the LDS Church (and the most married man in America).

Calls to missionary work have always come with a price. In 1839, for example, Joseph called on members of the Quorum of the Twelve to go on missions to England. The men left family members who were deathly ill from malaria; in fact, some of the apostles were so ill themselves that they had to be lifted into their wagons to begin the journey. And then the apostles were away from their families for a year, the women and children left to fend for themselves. This kind of situation

WHY DID IT HAVE TO BE **500** PAGES?!

wasn't uncommon. Missions could separate men from their families for years at a time.

As recently as the 1930s, a Mormon man could be called on a mission at virtually any point in his adult life—even within days of marrying—to proselytize or build a church somewhere. Until the 1960s, newly married couples could be called on missions together.

HONEY, HOW DOES A TWO YEAR PROSELYTIZING HONEYMOON IN SAMOA SOUND?

Missions nowadays are much more standardized. If you are male, you are eligible to go on a mission at age 18, and you serve for two years. If you are female, you are eligible at age 19 and serve for 18 months. (The logic behind the age difference is that less hanky-panky is likely to happen between males and females of sufficiently different ages.) Once a single male has passed the age of 26, the Church will no longer consider him for a mission. Single females, on the other hand, are eligible for missionary service at any time after their 19th birthday

When non-Mormons think about missions, they often think about the sacrifice it entails. The missionary gives up two years (or 18 months) to live a Spartan, strictly regimented lifestyle. Missionaries are allowed little contact with their families. No dating, television, or movies are allowed. And they do *not* get paid for their efforts.

Yet these sacrifices barely register on the radar of most missionaries. From their earliest days in Primary, young Mormons sing, "I hope they call me on a mission, when I have grown a foot or two . . . to teach and preach and work like missionaries do." To them, missionaries are good-looking, confident, adventurous souls brimming with exciting stories. The most exhilarating sacrament meetings are the ones where returned missionaries recount the "best two years" of their lives, sharing tales of miraculous occurrences, dramatic conversions, answered prayers, and giant banana spiders. The tales become so familiar that they take on a mythic quality, causing younger Mormons to think, "One day *I'll* get to be a missionary, too!"— much the way other kids think, "One day *I'll* get to be a superhero, too!"

Becoming a missionary requires two things: a basically clean (or rehabilitated) moral slate, and a means of support. Actual knowledge of the scriptures or Mormon doctrine isn't taken into much consideration when someone is being considered for a call. Essentially, if a person has the desire to serve and is worthy, it's a done deal. All that's left is to find out where the new missionary is going.

Probably the most electrifying moment in a young Mormon's life is when that chunky envelope from Church headquarters finally arrives. It will define not just one's next two years, but often one's entire life. Many families wait until the whole extended family can be gathered together, whether in person or via technology, before allowing the prospective missionary to open the letter. And then, after a brief salutation, the location is announced. Thailand? Argentina? Russia? Idaho? It could be anywhere. And for better or worse, that area becomes a huge part of that young Mormon's identity.

IT... IT'S HERE!

The months leading up to the missionary's departure are full of celebration and excitement: the buying of clothing and other essentials, the receiving of advice from returned missionaries, and goodbyes from family and friends. Then, on the scheduled day, the new missionary's parents drive to a drop-off lane at the assigned Missionary Training Center (MTC), where fellow missionaries unload the baggage (Mom and Dad don't get out of the car) and take the greenhorn to his or her first day of service.

There are more than a dozen MTCs throughout the world, from New Zealand to Ghana; the largest is in Provo, Utah. They're kind of like gospel boot camps, where missionaries sleep in barrack-like rooms and eat in a cafeteria, but spend the rest of their time packed into classrooms where the basics of the gospel and missionary work are drilled into their heads. Those who are not learning a new language spend three weeks in the MTC; new language-learners spend nine weeks.

Immediately upon entering the MTC, the new missionary is assigned a companion. This is the beginning of two years of never being alone except when going to the bathroom or taking a shower. Another missionary is always nearby. This snug arrangement can be beneficial, like when one is walking down a dark, inner-city alley; but it can also be annoying, like when one finds out that one's companion snores. Every once in a while, a missionary companionship will develop into a close friendship; other companionships can test a missionary's resolve to keep that pesky "thou shalt not kill" commandment.

By most standards, an LDS mission is a thoroughly unique experience. Few other cultures make room for their members to

take a two-year leave from the world. Most LDS missionaries head into the field propelled by two basic convictions: 1) that they are called to a specific place by God to make contact with people they are uniquely qualified to convert; and 2) that "the field is white, already to harvest"—in other words, that many people around them have been divinely prepared to join the church and that all the missionaries need to do is find them.

From Day One, Mormon missionaries are taught that they will experience success in direct proportion to their obedience. And the world of LDS missionaries is *packed* with rules. They are expected to rise at a particular time, shower and dress by a partic-

ular time, study scripture during a particular hour, be out the door and proselytizing by a particular hour, be back by a particular hour, and be in bed by a particular time. And, no, that isn't all. Their style of dress and grooming is also mandated, as is the kind of music they can listen to and the books they can read (a very slim selection) and even the length of their meals. They are also given goals to meet: this many doors knocked, this many lessons taught, this many baptism challenges given, this many baptisms. A leader usually calls in the evening to get a report on those goals.

If missionaries voluntarily and conscientiously obey the never-ending rules that direct their lives, finding their way into a flow of unwavering obedience, they can divest themselves of worldly cares. The idea is that they become more spiritually sensitive than they ever were in their at-home lives, where jobs, school, play, and dating took up their time and mental bandwidth. Many Mormons have said that the mission was the high watermark of their lives. Never again would they have the opportunity to experience the blessings of single-minded obedience.

Not every Mormon missionary takes the rules so seriously, but the intensive two-year training in obedience is a significant influence on most Mormons' lives, both religious and secular. Their willingness to take orders and defer to authority, along with immersion in a second language, makes them great recruit material for the CIA and FBI, which have higher-than-average Mormon populations.

And of course not everyone has the same mission experience. Some thrive on the military structure, some get a charge out of talking with strangers all day about the gospel, and some appreciate the opportunities for service. Others may find the constant interaction with strangers exhausting or their creativity stifled by the omnipresent rules, though they may appreciate the friendships they can cultivate with mission companions and potential converts.

But ask any Mormon you meet—even the ones who are disaffiliated from the Church—if they regret serving a mission. The great majority will say that they don't. Even if they are no longer believers, their missions still represent an important part of their lives—one in which they developed discipline and largeness of soul, and learned to love people they never would have connected with otherwise: the immigrant, the aged, the destitute, the ill, the grieving, the dying.

Some missionaries find that they are unable to meet the demands of the work—whether because of an illness or accident that occurs during their mission, or because of a pre-existing condition—and must leave their labors early. Missionaries who return prematurely often feel a sense of failure, as if they did not have sufficient faith to make it through their full term. A mission is a major part of a Mormon's identity. It isn't uncommon for newly introduced Mormons to ask each other, "Where did you go on your mission?" Having not completed the experience may make early-returned missionaries feel as though they have a secret to hide.

The Church does offers service missions, giving people an opportunity to work in a temple or various Church organizations rather than going out to proselytize. And it's not just the young women and men who serve missions. Retired couples are also a big part of the missionary force, though they often spend most of their time filling support and administrative roles, rather than proselytizing. And, like the younger missionaries, couple missionaries must support themselves.

TEMPLES

Temples are another kind of missionary work: the kind aimed at the deceased.

A core Mormon doctrine is that the human race is one big family, sharing a common Heavenly Parentage to whom we are striving to return. In order to make it back to them, however, we need to receive saving ordinances performed by someone with the proper authority. And those ordinances have to be performed physically.

This is a real bummer for most people who have lived on the earth because, well, they're dead.

Literally billions of people have had the bad luck of not living nearby when any of the dispensations of the gospel were made in the past. To compound the problem, even more billions are living on the earth *right now* who will never encounter the truth. Each and every one of these people, according to the LDS Church, needs these saving ordinances.

And that's what temples are for. They're the place where Mormons perform the herculean task of making up for thousands of years of apostasy by giving every single child of God a chance at receiving his or her temple ordinances by proxy.

Joseph Smith received his mission to "redeem the dead" when Elijah appeared to him in the Kirtland Temple, saying:

> 14 Behold, the time has fully come, which was spoken of by the mouth of Malachi—testifying that he [Elijah] should be sent, before the great and dreadful day of the Lord come—

> 15 To turn the hearts of the fathers to the children, and the children to the fathers, lest the whole earth be smitten with a curse —
>
> 16 Therefore, the keys of this dispensation are committed into your hands; and by this ye may know that the great and dreadful day of the Lord is near, even at the doors. *(D&C 110: 14–16)*

In other words, by doing temple work, Mormons stave off a curse prophesied in Malachi (*yay, Mormons!*) and, at the same time, usher in the great and dreadful day of the Lord (*uh, hold on there, Mormons*).

Temple Ordinances

Before performing ordinances for deceased ancestors, living Mormons need to receive their own. These ordinances are said to bestow great spiritual power and resources, so they are given to young Mormons just before they go on their missions to prepare them for the challenge.

To get into the temple, however, one needs to pass a temple-recommend interview, which consists of 15 questions designed to ascertain one's belief in core doctrines and how well one is keeping the basic commandments. Among the questions are the following:

+ Do you believe in God, Jesus Christ, and the Holy Ghost?
+ Do you support Church leaders?
+ Do you keep the law of chastity?
+ Are you honest?
+ Do you keep the Word of Wisdom?
+ Do you pay your tithing?

If the interviewee passes the test, the interviewer will sign a credit-card-sized "temple recommend" that allows the holder to participate in ordinances in any temple in the world.

The temple ordinance called the "endowment" is in many ways the pinnacle of the Mormon worship experience. Whereas the baptism and confirmation received earlier in life washed away sins and bestowed the gift of the Holy Ghost, the endowment kicks things up another notch—or 20—by cleansing initiates "from the blood and sins of this generation" and anointing them "kings and queens, priests and priestesses to the most high God."

The ceremony usually lasts about two-and-a-half hours: from the initiatory until the newly endowed member walks into the celestial room. It's a complex and often overwhelming ceremony, teeming with narrative, symbolism, covenants, and changes in clothing.

Convincing a Mormon to talk about the endowment ceremony is usually pretty difficult. Parts of it—such as the signs, tokens, and covenants—are protected by oaths that used to involve violent consequences for those who divulged them. (Now you simply draw down the wrath of God—which can be dangerous enough.) The rest of the ceremony is technically available to be discussed, but most Mormons consider it too sacred to talk about with people who aren't "spiritually prepared." Often they will not even speak about it with each other unless they are in the temple. And there's a kind of wisdom to this reticence. Jesus, after all, told his disciples that most of his words could be understood only by those "with ears to hear." Matters of great spiritual import require a kind of understanding not related to rationality, which is why spiritual teachings in most faiths are often presented as metaphors or symbols. And the Mormon temple is *full* of metaphors and symbols.

The Endowment Ceremony: An Inside Look

With all that in mind, the following is a brief description of the non-protected parts of the endowment ceremony. All of this information is available in public LDS Church documents. (No oaths were broken in the publication of this material!)

First, the initiate receives "initiatories," meaning that he or she is washed clean of the "blood and sins of this generation" and anointed  to become a king or queen, priest or priestess to God. For a long time, this rite was carried out while the initiate was covered by only a body shield (like what you might wear at a barbershop) and naked underneath. These days, the initiate is clothed during the ceremony. The officiator uses water and consecrated olive oil to anoint and bless the initiate. Men perform the rite for men, women for women.

When the washing and anointing is complete, the officiator authorizes the garment that the initiate is wearing (which was provided to them earlier). This is the "holy underwear" that so many people are curious about (though calling it "holy underwear" or "magic underwear" is definitely offensive to most Mormons). While a lot of folklore is handed around about how the garments protect their wearers from physical harm (and certainly many Mormon leaders have taught this idea), the Church currently emphasizes that the garments serve as *spiritual* protection and symbolize the wearer's fidelity to temple covenants and God.

After the initiatories, the initiate goes into a small room to receive a new name. This name is to be kept completely confidential until it is requested at the temple veil.

As is the case in rites of passage around the world, the endowment ceremony rehearses the group's story of stories—the creation of the earth, and the actions of key ancestors and cultural figures. In the case of LDS temples, initiates are immersed in God's creative acts and purposes for creation and follow Adam and Eve's time in the Garden of Eden, their fall, and their journey back to God.

The ceremony is a bit like interactive theater—or more often, interactive cinema. Everyone is seated on one side or the other of a small auditorium (based on gender), with an altar at the front. In the "live" temples (Manti and Salt Lake), live officiators perform the endowment story; in all other temples, the story is presented on film. The story begins with Jehovah and Michael creating the earth under Elohim's direction. (In an early version of the film, snippets of Disney's *Fantasia*—from "The Rite of Spring"—were used to illustrate the creation process. Since then the Church has produced its own special effects.)

Then the story of Adam and Eve is presented: their time in the Garden of Eden, their temptation by Satan, their partaking of the fruit of the Tree of Knowledge of Good and Evil, and their expulsion from the Garden. Eventually, Peter, James, and John (Jesus's disciples) come down to give Adam and Eve guidance as they navigate the "lone and dreary world."

At various points during the story, the action stops and an officiator comes to the altar to present a covenant that everyone in the audience must accept before the ceremony can move forward. The covenants come with "signs and tokens"—symbols and gestures—that the initiate must present at the end of the ceremony. Many Latter-day Saints find it ennobling that, just as God made individual covenants with prophets in the Hebrew Bible, they, too, are given this chance. At each covenant, they and the officiators representing God affirm these mutual promises individually.

Going through the endowment ceremony in one of the "live" temples is always an interesting experience. Only in these two temples does the audience move from room to room as the story's setting changes. For example, the creation of the earth will take place in the

"creation room," where painted planets and stars swirl across the walls. Then the audience will move into a room painted like the Garden of Eden, then into the "lone and dreary world," and then into the terrestrial and celestial rooms. In all other temples, the audience remains in one room for the entire ceremony, the shifts in story setting indicated by an announcement or by a change in lighting.

The participants start the ceremony dressed in white. As it progresses, they put on a green apron sewn with the shapes of leaves (as Adam and Eve present themselves before God after the fall), and then, when making various covenants, the "robes of the holy priesthood."

Toward the end of the ceremony, participants gather around the altar to enter the "true order of prayer," where they pray for, among other things, people listed on the temple's "prayer roll" of the sick and the struggling. As late as the 1970s, these prayer circles were also held outside the temple by ward and stake members; then, with the dramatic increase in temples around the world, the decision was made to confine prayer circles to temples.

The endowment is an ascension narrative representing a journey through life and offering opportunities for initiates to respond properly to archetypal challenges. This journey reaches its climax at the temple veil. There, the initiate gives each of the signs and tokens to someone standing on the other side of the veil, receives blessings in return, and finally is admitted through the veil into the "presence of God." Then the initiate enters the "celestial room," a large, well-appointed living room where he or she can sit and meditate on the endowment experience.

The Sealing: Marriage

For most Mormons, the final temple rite is the sealing: the Mormon term for marriage. In Mormonism, marriage isn't just "until death do us part"; it is "for time and all eternity."

To be sealed, a couple kneels on either side of an altar in a brightly lit "sealing room" lined with mirrors. As family members look on (those who have temple recommends, anyway), the sealer conducts the rite as the bride and groom hold each other's hands across the altar.

It's a simple ceremony, usually preceded by a sermon the sealer may feel inspired to deliver. But the sealing is an all-important capstone ordinance. As God declares in Doctrine and Covenants 132:

[I]f a man marry a wife by my word, which is my law, and by the new and everlasting covenant, and it is sealed unto them by the Holy Spirit of promise, by him who is anointed, unto whom I have appointed this power and the keys of this priesthood . . . they shall pass by the angels, and the gods, which are set there, to their exaltation and glory in all things, as hath been sealed upon their heads, which glory shall be a fulness and a continuation of the seeds forever and ever.

Then shall they be gods, because they have no end; therefore shall they be from everlasting to everlasting, because they continue; then shall they be above all, because all things are subject unto them (D&C 132:19–20)

In other words, marriage is essential to gaining the highest degree of heaven. Those who achieve this rank become like our Heavenly Parents, capable of producing spiritual children for eternity. (We have no details as to how spirit children are created, but if it's anywhere close to how mortals reproduce, we can only hope that heavenly pregnancy is a lot more fun.)

Very infrequently, married couples may receive a "second anointing" through a temple rite involving the washing of feet. But this ceremony is rarely performed these days and is typically reserved for high-ranking Mormon leaders.

Saving Ancestors

As pointed out at the beginning of the section, a great majority of the people who have lived on earth have not received these temple ordinances. Thus they cannot enter the Celestial Kingdom. After they die, they are relegated to "Spirit Prison," where they wait to be taught the gospel. If they accept the gospel, then they must wait for the temple ordinances to be done for them on earth.

For most Mormons, "temple work" for the dead starts with a single piece of paper, usually called a "four-generation pedigree chart." Children and teens are encouraged to fill out one of these sheets for themselves, partly to find out who their ancestors are and partly to find out if any of those ancestors are missing their

ordinances. Perhaps great uncle Earl was baptized but never received his endowment. Perhaps great-great grandma Lena was never sealed to her husband. Perhaps an aunt moved to Mozambique and changed her name. You have to go back and check; things can slip through the cracks.

Those who happen to find someone in their ancestral line who is missing ordinances become a kind of savior to them, doing something for the dead that they don't have the power to do for themselves: physically receive temple ordinances for them by proxy. It's pretty easy to find Mormons with a story about miraculously stumbling across a lost ancestor's name (especially

during the pre-Internet era, when just the right genealogy book fell off the shelf, or a specific cell of microfiche got caught in the machine's display window) and how they felt the spiritual presence of that person while performing temple ordinances for them. As they go through each ordinance—baptism, confirmation, initiatory, endowment, and sealing—many Mormons can feel that particular ancestor being freed from Spirit Prison and finally gaining access to Spirit Paradise.

Of course, there's also the other end of the spectrum: the stories of impatient ancestors appearing in order to berate a slothful descendant for not doing their temple work.

Most born-and-bred Mormons don't actually go inside a temple until they are teenagers. Even then, they are allowed only in the baptistery, where they do "baptisms for the dead." Only after they've received their own endowments (usually just before they go on a mission or get sealed) do they start to perform other ordinances for the dead. Really the only reason someone might go into the temple before their 12th birthday is if their family has recently converted and is getting sealed, or if they have been adopted and are getting sealed to their new family.

Temple work for the dead is a strange mix of the sacred and the industrial. First, everyone wears the same thing. A high-powered lawyer in an Armani suit and a migrant worker in overalls both may enter the temple locker room, but when they exit they will both be wearing exactly the same Church-produced outfit. The temple is meant to be an egalitarian space where all exterior differences drop away, emphasizing that "all are alike unto God."

NICE SUIT, MAN!!!

When conducting baptisms for the dead, one descends into a font built on the backs of twelve statues of oxen (meant to symbolize the Twelve Tribes of Israel), and then gets dunked dozens of times as the priesthood holder rapidly recites the baptism prayer, inserting the dead person's name at the right spot. Then one changes and enters a room where a series of confirmations happens just as fast; the priesthood holders lower their hands to one's head and then raise them after each ordinance is finished. Initiatories and sealings for the dead have a similar quickstep feel.

The only ordinance that doesn't seem rushed is the endowment, which always moves at a stately pace, usually dictated by video and

audio recordings. However, even as one performs the endowment on behalf of a deceased person, it is also meant to be a time to ponder one's own temple cove-nants, whether they had been made years ago or just yesterday. Thus, those going through the ceremony for the dead are usually mixed in with those who are receiving their endowments for the first time.

For many non-Mormons, temple ceremonies can seem strange, even a little sinister. But from an anthropological perspective, the temple ceremony is utterly normal. Tribal, religious, and fraternal cultures across the globe have used similar rituals for thousands of years to initiate young people into adulthood, to pass on knowledge, and to promote cultural cohesion. If these kinds of rituals are rare in secu-lar, Western cultures today, they live on in many tribal societies and religious traditions.

Non-Mormons may also feel that Mormons disrespect their ances-tors by trying to make them into Latter-day Saints after they're dead. For example, the American Gathering of Holocaust Survivors has been trying to get the LDS Church to remove the names of Jewish Holocaust victims from its genealogical databases for decades. Although the Church has complied in many ways, the names always seem to sneak back into the databases, reigniting the controversy. Even the Catholic Church has sometimes restricted Mormons from accessing its records for similar reasons.

Mormons will tell those bothered by temple work that they are simply *offering* the ordinances to the dead, and that the dead are under no obligation to receive them. This is technically correct, but it's also true that Mormons tend to think of temple ordinances as a kind of

missionary work, uniting all souls to God. In other words, they're usually confident that the ordinances *will* be received.

On the other hand, Mormons are sometimes bothered when non-members bring up the resemblances between temple ceremonies and Masonic rituals. It's true that Joseph Smith, his brother Hyrum, and his father all were Freemasons. It's also true that Joseph Smith went through a period of intense interaction with Masonry before he introduced the endowment and that many Masonic symbols and articles of clothing have been adapted for use in Mormon temple ceremonies.

The origins of Mormonism's most sacred rituals raise the question of whether truth and its practice must be created *ex nihilo* (out of nothing) or if they can be built from the materials at hand. It seems as though Joseph felt the second to be true.

FAMILY

From the discussion of temples, it is easy to see the theology that informs the Mormon emphasis on family. Earthly families are microcosms of the great heavenly family from which the earth's inhabitants originate. Earthly families are also the beginnings of the vast spiritual families that faithful Mormons will raise in the Celestial Kingdom. As Joseph Smith revealed, "that same sociality which exists among us here will exist among us there [in heaven], only it will be coupled with eternal glory." (D&C 130:2) In other words, for Mormons, getting married and raising a family isn't simply a way to perpetuate one's genes. It's the beginning of an eternities-long enterprise of producing spirit children and helping them to achieve exaltation so they can help *their* spirit children down the same path, and on and on.

The idea of marital units persisting into the eternities is taken very literally in Mormonism. As the Mormon poet (and one of Joseph Smith's plural wives) Eliza R. Snow once wrote, "In the heavens are parents single? No, the thought makes reason stare! Truth is reason truth eternal tells me I've a mother there." And as Donny Osmond writes on his website "[I]n the Celestial Kingdom ... husbands and wives ...

are the eternal unit, which will literally 'live' in the same house."

Currently, Mormonism focuses on the heterosexual, nuclear

family as "the fundamental unit of society." (*Ensign*, November 1995) And it puts a great deal of time, energy, and resources into supporting that unit. It holds Sunday school classes on parenting and family relationships, and it sets aside every Monday night for Family Home Evening, at which family members teach each other gospel principles, join in an activity, and share a treat. Every month, home teachers visit members' homes to make sure that all is well with the family.

Some readers may remember television ads by the LDS Church during the 1970s, 1980s, and 1990s that emphasized family values—such as the one showing a small boy trying to get the attention of his distracted mother by asking what she is writing in her planner. "The names of important people," she says. "Is my name in there?" he asks. Another ad, called "How to Grow Love in Your Own Front Yard," depicted a day in the life of an upper-middle-class Caucasian family in time-lapse photography, riding bikes, arm wrestling, taking pictures, and blowing bubbles in a hammock.

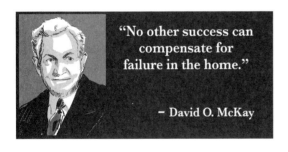

"No other success can compensate for failure in the home."

— David O. McKay

"No other success can compensate for failure in the home," said LDS Church president David O. McKay (1951–1970). This is a mantra Mormons try to live by. Even if the afterlife doesn't go exactly the way Mormons think it will, there is little doubt that their focus on building loving family relationships has brought much good into the world.

But the Mormon emphasis on the heterosexual, nuclear family comes with a complex history and a fraught future. The same revelation in the Doctrine and Covenants that reveals the eternal nature of the marriage relationship also reveals polygamy. Joseph Smith would sometimes get polygamously sealed to women who were already married, putting everyone concerned into a polyandrous relationship

(multiple men being married to one woman). Joseph and Emma Smith adopted a pair of twins after the infants' mother died in childbirth, and the twins were sealed to both the Smith family *and* their original mother and father. Sometimes families in the early Church would seal themselves to Joseph Smith's family, joining an already mind-bogglingly complex matrix of relationships. In other words, the monogamous, nuclear family wasn't the only family Joseph Smith had in mind when he talked about sealing. It was probably something closer to what his nephew Joseph F. Smith described: "There has got to be a welding together and a joining together of parents and children and children and parents until the whole chain of God's family shall be welded together into one chain." (*Millennial Star*, October 4, 1906)

Mormon divorce can get messy—theologically as well as domestically—pretty fast. What happens to a family if the parents get their sealing canceled? To whom are the children sealed, if at all? If the parents get sealed in the temple to other spouses, to which couple are the original children sealed? Church leaders assure members caught in such situations that everything will be sorted out in heaven, but give few clues as to how it will happen.

And speaking of complicated marriages, marrying outside the faith is a difficult thing indeed. Mormons who marry non-Mormons or who do not have their marriage sealed in the temple will basically be free-floaters in the eternities, unable to enter the highest levels of the Celestial Kingdom. Their marriages end at death and cannot be sealed except later in the temple by proxy. And any children they have will not be sealed to them. For this reason, Mormons are strongly encouraged to marry, as President Gordon B. Hinckley (1995–2008) put it, "the right person in the right place at the right time." (*Ensign*, February 1999)

The emphasis on family, however, also creates a forgotten sub-class of Latter-day Saints: singles. Singles wards are set up on college campuses and other populated areas for the express purpose of helping unmarried Latter-day Saints find eternal mates—and soon. As apostle Richard G. Scott once warned, "If you are a young man of appropriate age and are not married, don't waste time in idle pursuits. Get on with life and focus on getting married. Don't just coast through this period of life." (General Conference, April 2011) Such admonitions have been preached since the early days of the Church; in 1849 apostle Orson Hyde wrote, "That man who resolves to live without woman,

and that woman who resolves to live without man, are enemies to the community in which they dwell, injurious to themselves, destructive to the world, apostates from nature, and rebels against heaven and earth. (*Frontier Guardian*, Kanesville, Iowa, August 9, 1849)

There certainly have been prominent single people in the LDS Church, such as Steve Young when he was quarterback for the Denver Broncos; Sheri Dew, the CEO of Deseret Book, the LDS Church's publishing arm; and Evan Stephens, who first brought the Mormon Tabernacle Choir to national attention in the late 19th century. But in truth there is only a supporting role in Mormon theology for singles: they will be angels that serve deified couples in the Celestial Kingdom (though there is always the possibility of getting married in the next life).

With Mormon theology's heavy emphasis on producing large families both on earth and in heaven, it is also difficult to find a role for same-sex marriage. Since the whole purpose of deification is to multiply and replenish, same-sex couples wouldn't seem to have a place. Some Mormon thinkers have pointed out that there is nothing in the scriptures explicitly stating that deified couples reproduce sexually or that a male-female couple is required to "organize" a spirit. But the heterosexual union

is all-important in Doctrine and Covenants 132, where the marriage requirement for exaltation is laid out. Echoing its response to the plight of singles, LDS discourse suggests that homosexual orientation may drop away with the death of the mortal body, freeing those who were homosexual in mortality to marry heterosexually in the next life.

All in all, to be sure, Mormonism has had a complex, shifting relationship with marriage, practicing multiple forms of it over the course of its history. The Church has changed its position on polygamy and on interracial marriage as well. As one scholar noted, "a warning against racial intermarriage (ironically) was included on the front page of the very issue of the *Church News* containing the story of the [1978] revelation ending the priesthood restriction—as though to warn the Saints that just because blacks were getting the priesthood did not mean that intermarriage was acceptable!" (Armand Mauss, *Sunstone*, Summer 2015) Today, however, racial intermarriage is entirely acceptable, showing that the Church *does* shift. Someday it may even shift its perspective on same-sex marriage, though a lot of theological groundwork would need to be laid first.

MORMON MARRIAGE THROUGH THE AGES	19TH CENTURY	20TH CENTURY	21ST CENTURY	22ND CENTURY
	😄	🙂	🙂	🙂❓
	😛	😠	😠	😠❓
	😠	😐	🙂	🙂❓
	😠	😠	😠	🙁❓

part 4

HOT-BUTTON ISSUES

MOST OF THE HOT-
BUTTON ISSUES *in this
section revolve around identity
and the place of minorities and
marginalized people in Mormonism.
The growth of the Church, along with
the influence of the Internet, have
made more people from more diverse
backgrounds willing to speak up in what
has historically been a very white, very
patriarchal, very heterosexual Church.
But LDS membership is becoming much
more diverse, which means that the
Church inevitably must make room for
the various groups claiming a place at
the Mormon table.*

RACE AND THE PRIESTHOOD

Elijah Able

Ordained to the
Mormon Priesthood
before the
racial ban.

Though there are records of at least two black men being ordained to the priesthood in the early Church, the LDS Church had a policy from around 1852 to 1978 that banned people of black African descent from holding the priesthood or attending the temple. For a very long time, this policy fit squarely into the mainstream of white American racial thought. No churches run by Caucasians were ordaining blacks to their priesthoods, with most of them citing the curse and Cain and Ham as precedent. Mormonism was solidly on this scriptural bandwagon, but added a twist of its own: some Church leaders taught

Joseph Freeman

First African American
to be ordained to the
Mormon priesthood
after the racial ban
was rescinded.

that people who were born black had been fence sitters during the pre-mortal "war in heaven" and were therefore cursed in mortality. Many LDS leaders taught that blacks would not receive the priesthood or temple blessings until the Second Coming of Christ.

As the American civil rights movement began to gain momentum in the mid–20th century, some LDS members and leaders began to ask questions about the policy. But by now, the Church had accumulated more than a century's worth of culture and precedents, many of them assumed to be based in revelation or doctrine. A large church, like a large ship, needs time to turn—and that turning could not start

Jane Elizabeth Manning James

Early African American Convert.

"I try in my feeble way to set an example for all."

until there were enough people on board who were open to such a course correction.

There were a few times when it seemed that the Church was on the brink of dropping its ban on African American priesthood holders, but precedent has long dictated that all members of the First Presidency and Council of the Twelve must come to a consensus on matters of Church policy. President Spencer W. Kimball (1973–1985) had to talk with these leaders about the ban for years before finally achieving consensus in June 1978.

The language of the announcement is telling: "[God] has heard our prayers, and by revelation has confirmed that the long-promised day has come when every faithful, worthy man in the Church may receive the holy priesthood." In other words, God had "confirmed" the correctness of the principle the apostles had crafted through research, discussion, and prayer. Human agency and questioning had revealed the will of God—much as they had during the early days of the Church when the revelations making up the Doctrine and Covenants were being received.

Although the ban is well behind the Mormon Church by now, its memory continues to pose an obstacle to converting black Americans. And it was not until 2013 that the Church officially acknowledged that the ban was rooted in 19th-century racist tropes rather than divine revelation. While the Church has made strides in rooting out racist rhetoric from LDS discourse, one still hears occasional bits of racist folklore invoked in church meetings, usually by elderly members who grew up while the ban was still in place. Nor has the lifting of the ban had much of an impact yet on the selection of upper-level LDS Church leadership, which is still overwhelmingly composed of white males.

WOMEN AND THE PRIESTHOOD

Talking about the racial priesthood and temple ban inevitably brings up other priesthood restrictions: those on women.

As of the publication of this book, women in the Mormon Church are barred from holding the priesthood. Organizationally, this means that they do not have direct access to Church resources or leadership positions. Religiously, this means that they cannot carry out ordinances such as blessing the sacrament, performing baptisms, or giving healing blessings.

As we saw in Part 1, Joseph Smith taught that people must have the priesthood in order to act in God's name. Thus, if someone has a leadership position in God's church, it is essential that that person hold the priesthood. Otherwise, the person's actions have no authority.

In 1842, while the Saints lived in Nauvoo, Illinois, Emma Smith, Joseph Smith's first wife, helped found the Female Relief Society of Nauvoo. Upon reviewing the society's

Emma Hale Smith: Founder of the Relief Society of Nauvoo.

proposed constitution and by-laws, Joseph Smith is reported to have said, "I will organize the women under the priesthood after a pattern of the priesthood." (Sarah Granger Kimball, "Auto-Biography," *Woman's Exponent* vol. 12, September 1, 1883) This has led some historians to believe that Smith was planning to establish a female priesthood organization. However, Emma started using the society's meetings to express her opposition to polygamy, which eventually led Joseph to suspend its meetings. He died soon after.

Relief Society women participated not just in service projects but also in charismatic spiritual prac-

tices such as speaking in tongues and giving each other healing blessings. The latter resembled priesthood blessings, with a laying on of hands, but their efficacy was understood to be based on faith rather than on the official power of the priesthood. The healing blessings continued as a quasi-official part of Mormon women's interactions with each other when the Saints migrated to Utah. They would often perform a ritual for a woman approaching childbirth, anointing parts of her body with oil and pronouncing blessings upon them.

But Church support for the practice slowly dwindled. It finally disappeared in 1946, when all healing blessings were put under the auspices of the priesthood. Currently, women do not perform any ordinances except for the female initiatories in the temple. If a woman feels in need of any kind of blessing, she is supposed to call on her closest male relatives or ward members to provide it.

Women have only ever had access to Church funds and resources through male priesthood leaders. Indeed, for a long time, they had little access to any visible roles in the Church system. From 1930 to 1984 women did not speak in general conference. They did not sit on the stand at general conference until 1980. They did not pray in sacrament meetings until 1978, or in general conference until 2013. Photos of female general auxiliary leaders were not displayed in the Church's Conference Center until 2014. And all Relief Society and Young Women's activities, though run by women, are still presided over by men.

Jean A. Stevens:
First woman to pray in the LDS Church's general conference.

It may sound like the LDS Church is deeply patriarchal, and many Mormons will agree with that assessment without the slightest hesitation. For them, it is the way God set up the Church. Many Mormon women say that they are fine with this structure and consider it inspired. They appreciate their clear-cut roles and the chance to focus their energies on activities they consider eternally important, such as motherhood. The Church supports them in this view, often preaching that the raising of children is much more important than having a career or performing church leadership roles. (Oddly, few Mormon men clamor for an equal opportunity to stay home and raise their children.)

A number of movements to give women more say in the Church have sprung up since the 1970s, including the Exponent II group (named after the Relief Society's defunct magazine) and the Mormon Women's Forum. Then, in a 1998 interview with Larry King, LDS Church president Gordon B. Hinckley started a new wave of Mormon feminism, probably inadvertently, when he said, "Well, [women] don't

Are *gender* roles **best** when *shared?*

hold the priesthood at the present time. It would take another revelation to bring that about. I don't anticipate it. The women of the
Church are not complaining about it." Some LDS women took this
as a hint from the prophet that they needed to start asking the questions that would eventually bring about "another revelation." They
launched organizations, such as Ordain Women, which reason that
the Church is missing out on the leadership talents of half its population; that the gender imbalance in LDS leadership blinds it to the
needs of the Church's women; that a male-only priesthood is not con-
sistent with the Mormon doctrine of a Heavenly Mother; and that
accepting women into the core of Church leadership, rather than only
into auxiliary parts, would have a profound impact on the Church's
ability to do good in the world.

In one way, the issue of women holding the Mormon priesthood
is very different from similar debates in other traditions. Most religious institutions grant the priesthood to only a very select group of

people who have completed courses of study, taken particular vows, or accepted particular roles in the community. But in the Mormon Church, *all* worthy males, age 12 and up, can hold the priesthood. And, as some LDS women have pointed out, this tradition means that the most irreverent, goofiest 12-year-old boy in the Church has more religious power and organizational influence than the wisest 60-year-old woman.

But bringing women into the priesthood on a similar basis would mean that pretty much *everyone* over the age of 12 would have the priesthood. What would such a move mean about the priesthood's role? Giving women the priesthood would probably necessitate a reconception of what the priesthood gives its bearer access to, both religiously and organizationally. Thus, reconceiving the role of the priesthood would be a monumental task involving just about every aspect of Church organization—which isn't to say that such

paradigm-shifting conversations haven't taken place successfully in the Church before.

The Church has taken a few steps toward involving women in leadership roles, such as forming co-ed mission leadership councils in 2013, and in 2015 adding females to high-level, previously all-male, leadership councils such as the Missionary Executive Council, the Family Executive Council, and the Temple and Family History Executive Council.

LGBT ISSUES

N either the Book of Mormon, nor the Doctrine and Covenants, nor the Pearl of Great Price has anything to say about homosexuality. In fact, the word didn't even enter public Church discourse until the middle of the 20th century, though some people had been disfellowshipped (the second-most severe disciplinary action, usually involving a loss of some privilege) or even excommunicated for alleged same-sex liaisons earlier in Church history.

Starting in the late 1950s, some Church leaders advocated psychiatric theories suggesting that homosexuality could be "cured" and produced publications toward that end. In 1976, a Ph.D. student at Church-owned Brigham Young University wrote a dissertation reporting the results of experiments on "aversion therapy"—the administration of electric shocks to male subjects to inhibit sexual response when shown photos of nude men. Aversion therapy has since fallen out of favor both in the scientific and LDS communities. However, a great deal of discourse continues in LDS circles about whether a person can be "cured" of same-sex attraction, and some organizations founded by Church members (though not officially sponsored by the Church) attempt to do just that. Recent official LDS sources have acknowledged that homosexual orientation likely has biological roots.

Carol Lynn Pearson:
Mormon LGBT advocate.

Although official Church publications encourage leaders and

members to show compassion toward those with same-sex attraction, the Church's political actions against the legalization of same-sex marriage have created an environment that many gay and lesbian Latter-day Saints experience as hostile. "Straight members have absolutely no idea what it is like to grow up gay in this Church," wrote Stuart Matis a few weeks before he committed suicide on the steps of an LDS chapel in 2000. "Imagine the young gay boy frightened to death to divulge his secret pain to his dad because he witnesses his dad tromping around the neighbor[hood] placing up [anti-gay marriage] signs. Imagine the young gay girl who listens to her mother profess her love for her as she writes a check to oppose 'those filthy homosexuals.'"

Mitch Mayne:
Openly gay Latter-day Saint who sponsors outreach efforts to LGBT Mormons

Indeed, the LDS Church has become known for leading the charge against the legalization of same-sex marriage in the United States. During the 2008 Proposition 8 campaign to amend the California constitution to define marriage as between a man and a woman, the Church put considerable pressure on California Mormons to donate generously to the campaign and volunteer to canvas neighborhoods. Mormons were on the forefront of similar campaigns in Hawaii, Alaska, and Arizona. In 2015, when the U.S. Supreme Court deemed state laws prohibiting same-sex marriage unconstitutional, the LDS Church sent out a letter to every congregation in the United States and Canada expressing its disappointment in the ruling and reaffirming that Church officers would not officiate in same-sex marriages. In 2015, however, the Church did support a Salt Lake City ordinance prohibiting housing and job discrimination based on sexual orientation.

Momma Dragons

A group of LDS mothers who publicly
support their LGBT children.

Despite the Church's pervasive rhetoric against same-sex marriage, according to official LDS handbooks, homosexuals technically have just as much standing in the Church as heterosexuals. As long as they obey the law of chastity (no sexual relations outside a monogamous heterosexual marriage), they can get a temple recommend, go on a mission, and serve in callings (except for the high-level ones, like bishop, that require a married person). Thus, homosexuals have two options if they want to remain a member of the Church: stay single and celibate, or marry heterosexually.

Although LDS rhetoric about homosexuality has softened over the years, in 2015, *Handbook 1* (an administrative manual for Church leaders) was updated to read that a disciplinary council is "mandatory" for anyone who is in a "same-gender marriage." Further, children whose primary residence is with a same-sex couple (or with someone who has previously lived in a same-sex relationship) cannot receive any essential ordinances (such as baptism) until they are "of legal age," have moved out of their same-sex parents' household, and have "specifically disavow[ed] the practice of same-gender cohabitation and marriage." These children may participate in church meetings and activities, but not as full-fledged members. Because this is a policy and not a doctrine, however, it is subject to revision or even elimination. Though the majority of Mormons seemed to support the policy, a backlash developed that was significant enough for the *New York Times* to take notice and included a Salt Lake City event where more than 1,000 people resigned their Church membership.

BOOK OF MORMON HISTORICITY

From a Western, post-Enlightenment point of view, the claim that the Book of Mormon is an historical account of an ancient American people seems highly unlikely. The golden plates, from which the Book of Mormon is said to be translated, is not available for scholarly inspection. Moreover, according to the accounts, Joseph Smith didn't actually refer to the plates much during the translation process anyway—he received most of the Book of Mormon from gazing at a seer stone at the bottom of his hat. This is not the normal method for producing a reliable translation of an ancient record.

That said, the Book of Mormon has captured the religious imagination of millions of people, and one of the reasons it has done so is precisely *because* of its historical claims. Thus, from publication in 1830, the historicity of the Book of Mormon has been a major point of contention between Mormonism and its critics.

The debate is a rabbit hole that leads into rabbit holes that lead into rabbit holes. Summarizing its genres. complexities, and spin-offs would take an entire book of its own—and that book would soon be out of date, so quickly do the arguments and

...TIME FOR A LITTLE **LIGHT** READING!

counter-arguments proliferate. Perhaps the mere fact of such extensive discourse is a credit to the Book of Mormon. It means that the
book has the material, the mythos, and the complexity to provide fod-
der for such endless analysis.

The basic arc of historicity debates has been that early Church leaders, including Joseph Smith, made some very sweeping claims about
the civilizations described in the Book of Mormon, which, as scientific and archaeological evidence has grown, the Church and its apologists have had to qualify or reinterpret.

For example, the Church taught for a long time that the people of
the Book of Mormon—descended from Jewish immigrants—were
the "principal" ancestors of the American Indians. However, when
DNA studies found that the great majority of Native American DNA
was Asian in origin, the Church started teaching that the Book of
Mormon civilizations were "among" the ancestors of American Indians.

NATIVE AMERICANS

PRIMARY ANCESTOR

LAMANITES

It was also generally accepted in Church teachings that the civilizations in the Book of Mormon inhabited the entire Western Hemisphere. But analyses of Native American languages have caused the Church to lean toward a "limited geography" model,

LAMANITES   OTHER AMERICAN NATIONS

meaning that the Book of Mormon civilizations inhabited a much smaller area than originally taught.

There are also some details in the Book of Mormon that seem anachronistic, such as quotes from Isaiah that probably post-date the time the first Book of Mormon family left Jerusalem. There are also references to technologies (wheels, cement), flora (barley), and fauna (horses) for which there is no archaeological evidence from that time. In each of these cases, Mormon apologists have developed theories to explain or dismiss the critiques.

AHHHH ELBOW ROOM!

EXPANDED GEOGRAPHY MODEL

Mormon scholars from many disciplines have poured their energies into supporting the historicity of the Book of Mormon. Some have done word

HEY! WATCH THE ELBOWS!

LIMITED GEOGRAPHY MODEL

SHOVE OVER, MATE!

print analysis, some linguistic analysis, some geographic, some archae-ological, some cross-cultural, some anthropological, some scriptural, some medical—all producing fascinating, if esoteric, support.

Believing in the Book of Mormon's historicity—a literal reading—is a very important part of maintaining standing in the Church. Some who have publically argued against its historical authenticity have been disciplined or even excommunicated.

Though oceans of ink and untold resources have been poured into proving the Book of Mormon's historicity, the Church teaches that the most important "proof" of its status as scripture is its power to draw people closer to God. Does studying it improve one's life? Does it lead one be more compassionate and understanding? Does it lead one away from destructive behaviors? Does it bring one closer to the divine? Does God confirm its truth to one's heart? If so, the Church main-tains, then the Book of Mormon fulfills the most important func-tions of true scripture.

ONLINE ESSAYS

The LDS Church does seem to recognize the importance of addressing these and other challenges. Beginning in 2013, it started adding articles to its "Gospel Topics" webpage (www.lds.org/topics) that directly address controversial issues, including race and the priesthood, polygamy, DNA and the Book of Mormon, and violence in Mormon history. Considering that just a few decades ago some Mormons were disciplined or even excommunicated for publishing anything on these topics, these essays seem to signal an official trend toward greater openness.

part 5

THIS MORMON LIFE:

A NARRATIVE

W hile you will recognize some of the following concepts from previous parts of the book, this chapter will weave them together into an archetypal Mormon story. Probably the best way to understand Mormons from the inside—to see what they think about on a day-to-day basis, to see what drives them, to see what makes their lives meaningful—is to watch their journey from the very beginning to the very end.

And by "the very beginning" we mean the *very* beginning. We have to go *way* back. For example, you know those pictures of winged babies looking down from the clouds at their future parents? That's not far enough back. We have to rewind another few thousand eons, all the way back to a profoundly ancient time—even before the universe we live in came into existence—back to when humans were mere "intelligences."

Joseph Smith described intelligences as uncreated strains of refined matter, a kind of personal energy that has no beginning or end. They are as eternal as anything anywhere, including God.

Through some process, the Heavenly Parents (a.k.a. God) molded intelligences into their spiritual children. And all of these spirit children (i.e., you, me, everyone we know, and everyone else) "lived" with them for a long, long time. Some of them were "older," having been "born"

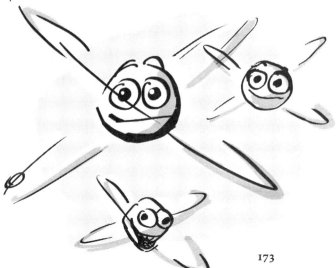

earlier, and some were younger. The first-born of the Heavenly Parents' children was named Jehovah (who would one day become Jesus Christ).

These spirit children were different from their Heavenly Parents in two significant ways. First, the Heavenly Parents had glorified physical bodies, while the spirit children had only spirit bodies. Second, they were quantum leaps more intelligent and more powerful than their children were. As the spirit children experienced the trials and possibilities of pre-mortality, they progressed and matured, but only to a particular point.

The Heavenly Parents wanted to give their offspring the opportunity to progress as far as they could. And, just as mortal children can grow to be as physically, mentally, and emotionally mature as their parents, so could spirit children. Yes, these spirit children had the potential to become gods.

But gaining that level of advancement required something frightening. The spirit children had to leave their Heavenly Parents' presence and show what kind of people they would be when left to themselves. They also had to experience a physical body with all its strengths and weaknesses.

So the Heavenly Parents put together a plan and presented it to their numerous progeny. They proposed that their children go down to an earth They would create and gain a physical body. But there was a catch. When entering a mortal body, a "veil" would be drawn between the heavenly sphere and the mortal world, leaving mortals without any memory of their time with their Heavenly Parents.

Of course, the Parents wouldn't completely abandon their children. They would provide "the light of Christ," which would beckon those who were listening toward goodness and soul-growth. But how each person responded to that invitation would be his or her own responsibility. Those who learned to follow the light, accept truth, and then spread the truth and light to others, could eventually return to the presence of their Heavenly Parents and be one step closer to becoming like them.

GREAT POWER

GREAT INTELLECT

PHYSICAL BODY

FLEDGING INTELLECT

LITTLE POWER

SPIRITUAL BODY

THE PLAN

EARTH

BODY

But Lucifer wouldn't let go of his idea and started what Mormons term "the war in heaven" (though it's often described as more of a knock-down, drag-out debate than an actual battle). It ended up that Lucifer swayed one-third of the spirits to his side while the other two-thirds sided with Jehovah.

The war finally reached such a pitch that Lucifer and his followers were cast down to earth. *But* they were denied mortal bodies and became tempters: the ones who, in a state of ravenous body-envy, try to lead the other two-thirds astray during their mortal term.

And so it is that every human who has lived on earth is part of the two-thirds that sided with Jehovah in the pre-mortal life. Yes, *everyone,* including Cain, Pontius Pilate, Vlad the Impaler, and Pol Pot. Even the inventor of bell-bottoms chose Jehovah in the beginning.

But there were some spirits who were especially valiant during the war. The Heavenly Parents saved them for the earth's last days, when the world would be at its most wicked, when it would be most

difficult to choose the right. And of these val-iant spirits, the Heavenly Parents chose only a few to be born into the Mormon Church, where they would be taught the truth from the very beginning. These spirits were the elect.

Indeed, Mormons are taught from early youth that they are

one of those double-whammied people—they carry a great honor, but also a great responsibility. Mormons have no excuses. God expects great things of them.

And now, finally, we get to mortal birth. Let's fol-low Michael and Mary here through their time in mortality.

The first thing to know is that these two get to start life 100 percent sin-free, along with the rest of human-ity. Most of Christianity teaches that, since Adam and Eve ate the fruit of the forbidden tree and were cast out of the Garden of Eden, they handed down their rebelliousness and sin through all genera-tions. But Mormonism's third article of faith bluntly states, "We believe that men will suffer for their own sins, and not for Adam's transgression."

So everyone starts as a blank slate. Any marks will be made by the person doing the sin-ning. In fact, everyone stays in this sinless state until age eight, which, in the Mormon Church, is when you're bap-tized. It's like getting a war-ranty on a new car. You get to test drive your body for eight

years before any infractions you commit actually stick.

Mormon parents and church leaders all work hard to make sure that children are ready for that landmark birthday. Parents may have weekly Family Home Evenings, where the family gets together to learn about the gospel and eat treats. They'll bring their kids to Primary every Sunday to sing songs about gospel principles and listen to lessons. They'll likely read the Book of Mormon to their children every night, leaving them with the stories of Nephi, Alma, and Ammon banging around in their little brains. They may have family prayer each morning and evening. They may encourage their children to say their own twice-daily prayers—plus meal prayers. The gospel can potentially saturate every aspect of a young Mormon's life.

And then the big day finally comes when the eight-year-old Mormon dresses in a white jumpsuit, steps down into the font with a priesthood holder (maybe his or her dad) and gets baptized. At which point, the sin scoreboard flashes on.

Right after baptism comes confirmation, where one officially becomes a member of the Church and receives the gift of the Holy Ghost, which intensifies the effects of the light of Christ.

Each Sunday after baptism, for the rest of their lives, Latter-day Saints take the sacrament (the Mormon version of communion) to renew their baptismal covenants. At age 12, the different roles boys and girls are assigned in the Church start to come to the fore. Boys receive the Aaronic priesthood and become deacons (which means they pass the sacrament and collect offerings, among other duties), while girls go into the Young Women's program. This is the training ground for gender roles in the Church. Men are expected to preside, both in church and at home. Women are expected to raise families and support their husbands in their priesthood callings. The emphasis on these roles varies from region to region, but throughout the church, men have the priesthood, and therefore the leadership roles, and women have "auxiliary" roles.

Mormon teens are kept very busy. Depending on where they live, they may have seminary classes every day, weekly Young Men and Young Women activities, and at least three hours of Sunday meetings—which is why Mormons always seem so busy.

This is probably all for the best because there are a lot of things Mormon teens aren't allowed to do, like have pre-marital sex, smoke cigarettes, drink alcohol (or even

coffee and tea), or use illicit drugs
Heck, often they can't even date
until they're 16. All of these
activities are quite tempt-
ing to hormone-ravaged
boundary-testing teenag-
ers, of course, but young
Mormons can't do any of it
because most of them are getting ready to go on a mission.

And they're *really* excited about their missions. Not just because
there's the possibility of living for two years in another country and
learning a new language, but because they get to follow in the footsteps of the great missionaries of old. They're told they will be like
St. Paul heading into Athens, or Ammon going to Lamanite lands, or
Brigham Young preaching in England. Or even like their own moms
and dads, who likely shared their mission stories. Going on a mission means leaving behind the life they've known—school, hobbies,
family, friends—and dedicating their full life to God. It sounds like
a sacrifice, but ask any Mormon about miracles they experienced on
their mission, and they will have stories for you.

Mormon missionaries aren't just trying to convince other people of the truthfulness of the gospel. They are attempting to gather
in God's spirit children—their spiritual brothers and sisters—and
remind them of the truths they once knew.

So off they go on their missions. Maybe to Japan, maybe to
Argentina, maybe to South Africa, maybe to Texas. They spend 18
months to two years talking to people in the streets, knocking on their
doors, doing service projects, visiting less-active church members, and
generally trying to make the world a better place. Most Mormons will
tell you that they experienced the best days and the worst days of their
lives while serving God. These are unforgettable years.

The first few weeks after returning from a mission are probably the strangest a Mormon ever experiences. They have to get used to thinking about their classes or their job or their taxes instead of what soul may be waiting to hear the gospel next.

But there is a big perk: they are also *returned missionaries*. And that's the biggest smiley face they can possibly have in their mating resume. The eyes of the opposite sex light up when they hear about one's "RM" status. They'll suddenly want to get to know this new possibility better. They'll flirt earnestly to see if this particular pairing is a good match: to see if eternal companionship could possibly be in the cards.

Because that's what Mormon marriage is all about: eternity. Most Christian and secular wedding ceremonies end with the words, "until death do us part." But in a Mormon wedding ceremony, phrases like "for time and all eternity" and "new and everlasting covenant" are used. This couple isn't just getting married; they're taking another step toward becoming like their Heavenly Parents. They're starting a trial run into godhood.

As the marriage ceremony ends, the couple is told to "multiply and replenish the earth and have joy and rejoicing in your posterity." This bit of advice is meant to remind them that a whole bunch of spirit children are still waiting for their turn at a mortal body. And the more that get born into the true church, the better. This is one of the reasons why Mormon families tend to be larger than average. They're giving as many spirits as possible their best chance at salvation.

Of course, just being born into a Mormon family doesn't ensure salvation. The plan of salvation turns on agency—on a person making constructive choices of his or her own volition. However, raising a child in righteousness can go a long way toward helping him or her down the right path.

With marriage and child rearing comes the long haul of Mormon adult life. One serves in one's local congregation in all kinds of callings:

perhaps Sunday school president one year, nursery worker the next. A male may become a bishop—the man who is in charge of the entire congregation—and a female may become Relief Society president—the woman who is in charge of all the women. An adult Mormon may even be called to serve in a stake position (one level up from the congregational level). But no one gets any special training for these callings, and no one gets paid either. Working for one's congregation is like working for God. And God often calls people to jobs that feel completely out of their depth. That is when they remember the verse in Ether that says, "I give unto men weakness that they may be humble . . . if they humble themselves before me, and have faith in me, then will I make weak things become strong unto them." (Ether 12:27)

Mormons tend to be unusually successful at their worldly pursuits. In the book *The Triple Package: How Three Unlikely Traits Explain the Rise and Fall of Cultural Groups in America* (2014), Amy Chua and Jed Rubenfeld posit that some cultural groups, including Mormons, tend to be more successful because they have three traits: a superiority complex, insecurity, and impulse control.

You have already seen where the superiority complex comes in. Not only do Mormons believe that they chose Jehovah in the pre-mortal life, but they also believe that, being born in the Mormon Church, they are incontestably one of God's elect. They weren't sent to earth just to live quietly, they were sent for a *purpose*.

The insecurity may seem a little less evident. But consider a verse from 2 Nephi: "we know that it is by grace that we are saved, after all we can do" (2 Nephi 25:23). Most Mormons are plagued with uncertainty when it comes to their salvation: they merit grace only after all they can do, but who knows how much *that* is?

Moreover, according to some Church leaders, most Mormons will actually end up in the "Terrestrial Kingdom," which is one step down from the "Celestial Kingdom" (the Mormon term

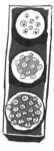

for heaven). Only the super righteous get into the Celestial Kingdom, and even *that* kingdom has three levels; it's only at the highest level that one becomes like God. In other words, I may be OK and you may be OK, but in no way does that mean that being OK is OK enough.

So, yeah, Mormons are insecure. They're never sure if they've done enough to earn the prize. There are always more meetings to go to, more children to have, more callings to fulfill, more temple sessions to attend. And this insecurity bleeds into their worldly pursuits. They want first prize there, too. Especially since the Book of Mormon promises prosperity to the righteous. In many ways, Mormons feel like their financial and professional successes are approximate mirrors of their spiritual success.

And so, when retirement comes, Mormons don't get to rest. Most likely, they'll start to get more church callings: a temple worker, a family history specialist, a branch president . . . a missionary. It's true. A Mormon's mission years are in no wise finished when they come home in their early twenties. They can be called again and sent just about anywhere, from Guatemala to Mongolia, though they usually don't do much direct proselytizing. They usually play supporting roles, strengthening new wards and branches, reactivating lapsed Church members, taking care of Church buildings, etc. And there's no limit to the number of missions an older couple can go on as long as they're healthy and have the financial resources. (Once again, they're not getting paid.)

And finally, death comes. But this is in no way the end; death is just a transition where the spirit exits the mortal body. Then, depending on how one has lived, one ends up either in Spirit Paradise or in Spirit Prison.

Spirit Paradise is a kind of resting area for those who have worn out their lives in God's service as they wait for the Final Judgment. Or not. Actually, Spirit Paradise is just a pit stop before the righteous are deployed to Spirit Prison to teach the people who didn't receive the gospel during mortal life, or who didn't live their lives well. And since the Mormon gospel has been available only for the past 200 years or so, pretty much the entirety of humanity is waiting for them.

No rest for the righteous.

Our information about the journey after this point gets pretty vague. It may be that eons will pass as post-mortal spirits continue to grow toward godhood. It may be that no one will get placed in one of the three kingdoms for a few more eternities. The one sure thing, according to Mormonism, is that everyone will eventually get resurrected, gaining a glorified body of flesh and bone, just like the ones the Heavenly Parents have. That's a gift that every single spirit that goes through mortal life is given. The rest is kind of fuzzy.

Some obscure Mormon sermons have taught that, in order to become a god, one has to go through the process of being a savior to a world, kind of like Jehovah/Jesus did for ours. Some Church leaders have even taught that gods are polygamous. (How else do all those spirit children get created?) Some say that moving up through kingdoms is possible, while others have insisted that once you've landed, you're stuck.

But all of that is minutiae. One's ultimate destiny depends entirely upon the kind of growth pattern one has established. Those who have learned to accept truth when it is presented, who are always looking for ways to improve themselves, who are learning to interact compassionately with other people, who are developing their own connection with the divine, are on the right trajectory. Where a person *is* at a particular moment isn't as important as where that person is *headed*.

Mormons hope that they will eventually find themselves in the same position the Heavenly Parents found themselves in so long ago: a heaven full of spirit children all champing at the bit, yearning for progression, excited to get out and test their mortal legs. They hope to make a world for them, and—trembling, anxious, full of hope— send them down to craft their souls, just as they themselves did so many eternities ago.

As the Mormon hymn proclaims:

The works of God continue,
  And worlds and lives abound;
  Improvement and progression
  Have one eternal round.

FURTHER READING

Alexander, Thomas G. *Mormonism in Transition: A History of the Latter-day Saints 1890–1930*. Salt Lake City, UT: Greg Kofford Books, 2012.

Argetsinger, Gerald S., Jeff Laver, and Johnny Townsend. *Latter-Gay Saints: An Anthology of Gay Mormon Fiction*. Maple Shade, NJ: Lethe Press, 2013.

Arrington, Leonard, and Davis Bitton. *The Mormon Experience: A History of the Latter-day Saints*. Urbana: University of Illinois Press, 1992.

Barnes, Jane. *Falling in Love with Joseph Smith: My Search for the Real Prophet*. New York: Tarcher, 2014.

Barlow, Philip. *Mormons and the Bible: The Place of the Latter-day Saints in American Religion*. New York: Oxford University Press, 2013.

Bigler, David L. *The Forgotten Kingdom: The Mormon Theocracy in the American West 1847–1896*. Spokane, WA: Arthur H. Clark, 1998.

Bowman, Matthew. *The Mormon People: The Making of an American Faith*. New York: Random House, 2012.

Brooks, Joanna, Rachel Hunt Steenblik, and Hannah Wheelwright. *Mormon Feminism: Essential Writings*. New York: Oxford University Press, 2015.

Brooks, Juanita. *The Mountain Meadows Massacre*. Norman: University of Oklahoma Press, 1993.

Buerger, David J. *The Mysteries of Godliness: A History of Mormon Temple Worship*. Salt Lake City, UT: Signature Books, 2002.

Bushman, Richard Lyman. *Joseph Smith: Rough Stone Rolling*. New York: Alfred A. Knopf, 2005.

Bushman, Richard Lyman. *Mormonism: A Very Short Introduction*. New York: Oxford University Press, 2008.

Card, Orson Scott. *Saints*. New York: Forge Books, 2001.

Compton, Todd. *In Sacred Loneliness: The Plural Wives of Joseph Smith*. Salt Lake City, UT: Signature Books, 1997.

Daynes, Kathryn M. *More Wives than One: Transformation of the Mormon Marriage System, 1840–1910*. Urbana: University of Illinois Press, 2008

Flake, Kathleen. *The Politics of American Religious Identity: The Seating of Senator Reed Smoot, Mormon Apostle*. Chapel Hill: University of North Carolina Press, 2004.

Givens, Terryl L. *By the Hand of Mormon: The American Scripture that Launched a New World Religion*. New York: Oxford University Press, 2002.

Givens, Terryl L. *People of Paradox: A History of Mormon Culture*. New York: Oxford University Press, 2007.

Givens, Terryl L. *Wrestling the Angel: The Foundations of Mormon Thought: Cosmos, God, Humanity*. New York: Oxford University Press, 2014.

Hallstrom, Angela, ed. *Dispensation: Latter-day Fiction*. Provo, UT: Zarahemla Books, 2010.

Haws, J.B. *The Mormon Image in the American Mind*. New York: Oxford University Press, 2013.

Homer, Michael W. *Joseph's Temples: The Dynamic Relationship between Freemasonry and Mormonism*. Salt Lake City: University of Utah Press, 2014.

Mauss, Armand. *All Abraham's Children: Changing Mormon Conceptions of Race and Lineage*. Urbana: University of Illinois Press, 2003.

Mauss, Armand. *The Angel and the Beehive: The Mormon Struggle with Assimilation*. Urbana: University of Illinois Press, 1994.

Newell, Linda King, and Valeen Tippetts Avery. *Mormon Enigma: Emma Hale Smith*. 2nd ed., Urbana: University of Illinois Press, 1994.

Ostling, Richard, and Joan K. Ostling. *Mormon America: The Power and the Promise*. Rev. ed., New York: HarperOne, 2007.

Peterson, Levi S. *The Backslider*. Salt Lake City, UT: Signature Books, 2012.

Prince, Gregory A. *David O. McKay and the Rise of Modern Mormonism*. Salt Lake City: University of Utah Press, 2005.

Reeve, W. Paul. *Religion of a Different Color: Race and the Mormon Struggle for Whiteness*. New York: Oxford University Press, 2015.

Schow, Ron, Wayne Schow, and Mary Beth Raynes. *Peculiar People: Mormons and Same-Sex Orientation*. Salt Lake City, UT: Signature Books, 1991.

Sorensen, Virginia. *Where Nothing Is Long Ago: Memories of a Mormon Childhood*. Salt Lake City, UT: Signature Books, 1999.

Steinberg, Avi. *The Lost Book of Mormon: A Journey through the Mythic Lands of Nephi, Zarahemla, and Kansas City, Missouri*. New York: Nan A. Talese, 2014.

Turner, John G. *Brigham Young: Pioneer Prophet*. Cambridge, MA: The Belknap Press of Harvard University Press, 2012.

Van Wagoner, Richard S. *Mormon Polygamy: A History.* Salt Lake City: Signature Books, 1989.

Walker, Ronald W., Richard E. Turley, and Glen M. Leonard. *Massacre at Mountain Meadows.* New York: Oxford University Press, 2011.

Whipple, Maureen. *The Giant Joshua.* Salt Lake City, UT: Western Epics, 1976.

Websites

Affirmation: LGBT Mormons, Families, and Friends: *www.affirmation.org*

Brigham Young University: *www.byu.edu*

BYU Studies: *byustudies.byu.edu*

The Church of Jesus Christ of Latter-day Saints: *www.lds.org*

The Church of Jesus Christ of Latter-day Saints, Scriptures: *www.lds.org/ scriptures*

The Church of Jesus Christ of Latter-day Saints, What LDS Members Believe: *www.mormon.org*

The Church of Jesus Christ of Latter-day Saints, Newsroom: *www. mormonnewsroom.org*

The Church of Jesus Christ of Latter-day Saints, Magazines: www.lds. org/magazine

Dialogue: A Journal of Mormon Thought: *www.dialoguejournal.com*

Encyclopedia of Mormonism: *eom.byu.edu*

FairMormon: *www.fairmormon.org*

Joseph Smith Papers: *josephsmithpapers.org*

Mormon History Association: www.mormonhistoryassociation.org

Mormon Matters: www.mormonmatters.org

Mormon Stories: www.mormonstories.org

Neal A. Maxwell Institute for Religious Scholarship: maxwellinstitute.byu. edu

PBS—*Frontline* and *American Experience,* "The Mormons": *www.pbs.org/ mormons*

Signature Books Online Library: www.signaturebookslibrary.org

Sunstone Magazine: www.sunstone.org

About the Author and Illustrator

STEPHEN CARTER, PH.D., is the editor of *Sunstone* (an independent Mormon magazine), the creator and co-author of iPlates (an award-winning series of graphic novels based on the Book of Mormon), a father of three, a husband of one, and the Sunday school president for his Mormon ward. Find more information about him at: *stephencarter.me.*

JEANETTE "JETT" ATWOOD is an animator and cartoonist who works primarily as a storyboard artist. She has extensive credits in comic books, video games, and short films, and collaborates with Stephen Carter on the iPlates series. Jett also spins plates, plays the trumpet a little, and is learning to juggle. You can see more of her work at *jettatwood.com.*

THE FOR BEGINNERS® SERIES

AFRICAN HISTORY FOR BEGINNERS   ISBN 978-1-934389-18-8
ANARCHISM FOR BEGINNERS   ISBN 978-1-934389-32-4
ARABS & ISRAEL FOR BEGINNERS   ISBN 978-1-934389-16-4
ART THEORY FOR BEGINNERS   ISBN 978-1-934389-47-8
ASTRONOMY FOR BEGINNERS   ISBN 978-1-934389-25-6
AYN RAND FOR BEGINNERS   ISBN 978-1-934389-37-9
BARACK OBAMA FOR BEGINNERS, AN ESSENTIAL GUIDE   ISBN 978-1-934389-44-7
BEN FRANKLIN FOR BEGINNERS   ISBN 978-1-934389-48-5
BLACK HISTORY FOR BEGINNERS   ISBN 978-1-934389-19-5
THE BLACK HOLOCAUST FOR BEGINNERS   ISBN 978-1-934389-03-4
BLACK PANTHERS FOR BEGINNERS   ISBN 978-1-939994-39-4
BLACK WOMEN FOR BEGINNERS   ISBN 978-1-934389-20-1
BUDDHA FOR BEGINNERS   ISBN 978-1-939994-33-2
BUKOWSKI FOR BEGINNERS   ISBN 978-1-939994-37-0
CHOMSKY FOR BEGINNERS   ISBN 978-1-934389-17-1
CIVIL RIGHTS FOR BEGINNERS   ISBN 978-1-934389-89-8
CLIMATE CHANGE FOR BEGINNERS   ISBN 978-1-939994-43-1
DADA & SURREALISM FOR BEGINNERS   ISBN 978-1-934389-00-3
DANTE FOR BEGINNERS   ISBN 978-1-934389-67-6
DECONSTRUCTION FOR BEGINNERS   ISBN 978-1-934389-26-3
DEMOCRACY FOR BEGINNERS   ISBN 978-1-934389-36-2
DERRIDA FOR BEGINNERS   ISBN 978-1-934389-11-9
EASTERN PHILOSOPHY FOR BEGINNERS   ISBN 978-1-934389-07-2
EXISTENTIALISM FOR BEGINNERS   ISBN 978-1-934389-21-8
FANON FOR BEGINNERS   ISBN 978-1-934389-87-4
FDR AND THE NEW DEAL FOR BEGINNERS   ISBN 978-1-934389-50-8
FOUCAULT FOR BEGINNERS   ISBN 978-1-934389-12-6
FRENCH REVOLUTIONS FOR BEGINNERS   ISBN 978-1-934389-91-1
GENDER & SEXUALITY FOR BEGINNERS   ISBN 978-1-934389-69-0
GREEK MYTHOLOGY FOR BEGINNERS   ISBN 978-1-934389-83-6
HEIDEGGER FOR BEGINNERS   ISBN 978-1-934389-13-3
THE HISTORY OF CLASSICAL MUSIC FOR BEGINNERS   ISBN 978-1-939994-26-4
THE HISTORY OF OPERA FOR BEGINNERS   ISBN 978-1-934389-79-9
ISLAM FOR BEGINNERS   ISBN 978-1-934389-01-0
JANE AUSTEN FOR BEGINNERS   ISBN 978-1-934389-61-4
JUNG FOR BEGINNERS   ISBN 978-1-934389-76-8
KIERKEGAARD FOR BEGINNERS   ISBN 978-1-934389-14-0
LACAN FOR BEGINNERS   ISBN 978-1-934389-39-3
LIBERTARIANISM FOR BEGINNERS   ISBN 978-1-939994-66-0
LINCOLN FOR BEGINNERS   ISBN 978-1-934389-85-0
LINGUISTICS FOR BEGINNERS   ISBN 978-1-934389-28-7
MALCOLM X FOR BEGINNERS   ISBN 978-1-934389-04-1
MARX'S DAS KAPITAL FOR BEGINNERS   ISBN 978-1-934389-59-1
MCLUHAN FOR BEGINNERS   ISBN 978-1-934389-75-1
MUSIC THEORY FOR BEGINNERS   ISBN 978-1-939994-46-2
NIETZSCHE FOR BEGINNERS   ISBN 978-1-934389-05-8
PAUL ROBESON FOR BEGINNERS   ISBN 978-1-934389-81-2
PHILOSOPHY FOR BEGINNERS   ISBN 978-1-934389-02-7
PLATO FOR BEGINNERS   ISBN 978-1-934389-08-9
POETRY FOR BEGINNERS   ISBN 978-1-934389-46-1
POSTMODERNISM FOR BEGINNERS   ISBN 978-1-934389-09-6
PROUST FOR BEGINNERS   ISBN 978-1-939994-44-8
RELATIVITY & QUANTUM PHYSICS FOR BEGINNERS   ISBN 978-1-934389-42-3
SARTRE FOR BEGINNERS   ISBN 978-1-934389-15-7
SAUSSURE FOR BEGINNERS   ISBN 978-1-939994-41-7
SHAKESPEARE FOR BEGINNERS   ISBN 978-1-934389-29-4
STANISLAVSKI FOR BEGINNERS   ISBN 978-1-939994-35-6
STRUCTURALISM & POSTSTRUCTURALISM FOR BEGINNERS   ISBN 978-1-934389-10-2
WOMEN'S HISTORY FOR BEGINNERS   ISBN 978-1-934389-60-7
UNIONS FOR BEGINNERS   ISBN 978-1-934389-77-5
U.S. CONSTITUTION FOR BEGINNERS   ISBN 978-1-934389-62-1
ZEN FOR BEGINNERS   ISBN 978-1-934389-06-5
ZINN FOR BEGINNERS   ISBN 978-1-934389-40-9